THE POWER OF THE LIGHT

Worship Services For Family Participation

Compiled and Edited by Ralph E. Dessem and D. Gary Klempnauer

THE POWER OF THE LIGHT

ISBN 0-89536-330-5   PRINTED IN U.S.A.

TABLE OF CONTENTS

INTRODUCTION

We find ourselves living in the midst of a changing society, in which some of the foundations of family life are rapidly decaying. Recent statistics reveal that one-third of all marriages in the United States now end in divorce, and one-sixth of all school age children live with a single parent. As American family life continues to deterioriate, the church is increasing its efforts to strengthen family solidarity. Clergy, as well as the majority of laypersons, are in agreement regarding the necessity of a strong spiritual foundation for family unity. Many programs have been developed within the church to accomplish this purpose.

Most authorities on family life emphasize the importance of all members of the family doing things together. From this has come the church's emphasis on family camping, family nights, and weekend family retreats. Unfortunately, in too many churches we have failed to guide the family in doing things together on Sunday morning. In fact, in many churches "segregation" begins at the front door! Little Sally is taken to the church nursery, Jimmy hurries to his elementary church school class, Mary finds her way to Junior Church and Larry attends the high school discussion group; of course, at the same time mother and father are in the worship service in the church sanctuary.

If it is important for members of the family to do things together, why shouldn't they worship together? We are learning the value of intergenerational experiences in Christian education. There is also much to be gained by each member of the family in intergenerational worship. However, for such services to be effective, they must include the participation of children and youth in experiences other than merely singing hymns and reading prayers.

This book contains models of worship experiences which can be used in intergenerational groups. Herein is presented a vast collection of ideas which have been placed in the context of worship experiences. We urge you to take these ideas seriously and give this book to creative persons interested in worship, drama, music, and education. You will soon discover a change occurring in the Christian community to which you belong. This book does not do the work — but it is a resource which will stimulate persons to create innovative worship experiences.

We would appreciate hearing from you in regard to what you have done. Let us know of your experiences which are successful as well as those that flop! Send us a tape or a letter to share the things you have developed in your own church situation. We can all benefit as together we endeavor to strengthen the family through worship.

Ralph E. Dessem

D. Gary Klempnauer

The Power of the Light

Theme of the Service
This service of worship is a celebration of:
...the Birth of God's Son
...the formal witness of the Three Kings
...the dramatic testimony of the Apostles, the
Saints, and the contemporary Church.
It is a service of light, portraying the word of God
illuminating the world. This service moves beyond the
life of Jesus to include the early church and the
contemporary church.
It is an exhilarating service of Scripture, music, and
light. Persons will respond enthusiastically to the
simplicity and the representation of the growth of the
church.

Directions for the Service
The Service of Lights has been used by many
churches to celebrate the Epiphany Season. This service
comes from the Episcopal tradition. Some churches
approach the service as a children's service; others mix
adults and children; others use adults. With the
emphasis upon intergenerational experiences the
Festival of Lights is contemporary. It lends itself to
participation of children, youth, and adults.
Rehearsal is necessary. However, the rehearsal may
be neatly accomplished in segments. The participants
need not sit through the whole program. In fact,
children will be more attentive if they have not had to
sit through a long rehearsal. Rehearse their entrance
into the Sanctuary. Show them which candles to light,
where to sit; that is enough.
It is extremely helpful to use the choir(s) of the
church in this service. The Service of Light has three
components of equal importance:

light
Scripture
music

The choirs and soloists will individualize the service and add to the drama of the experience.

The Scripture readings may be divided between liturgist and narrator, or all reading may be done by one person. (Two are preferred, possibly one adult and one youth.)

During the Fifth Lesson, three men come down the aisle(s) each singing one verse of the hymn, "We Three Kings." The Kings return up the aisle (leaving the Sanctuary) on the fifth verse or final refrain.

During the Sixth Lesson, the Judas Candle should burn during the singing of the first verse of the hymn. Then it should be extinguished to prepare for the Seventh Lesson.

Please Note: The candlelighter must be ready to move into position at the closing of the hymn and ready to light his candle(s) immediately, upon cue from the Narrator. If this is not done, the service will drag and much of the joy and sense of progression will be lost.

The director of the service might be tempted to use only two acolytes to light the candles. Of course this could be done. However, the drama of the processional would be limited. Second, fewer persons would be involved in the service. Generally, the service will be more effective using different persons for the acolytes in the various segments of the service.

The director of the service should be available to be certain that the acolytes do not lag or miss their entrance.

As the service concludes, candlelight will gradually fill the Sanctuary as the Scripture testifies to God's victory in the world. As persons leave the Sanctuary, they might desire to carry their lighted candles into the world, thus participating in carrying the symbol of God's Word into the world.

The Service begins in a dimly-lighted Sanctuary. After the first hymn, the lights of the Sanctuary are extinguished and the Christ Candle is lighted. From that point, electric lights are not used; the only available light comes from candles which are being lighted. However, if the hymns are not familiar to your congregation, it might be necessary to add illumination during the service. Candles could be placed in windows. If all else fails, utilize dim electric lighting which can be eliminated near the conclusion of the service. This matter must be carefully considered. Provide plenty of time to work out your light strategy.

Finally a word of caution about candles and fire restrictions. This service utilizes a great many candles. You will need to have some fire extinguishers handy and persons designated to use them. You might want to contact members of the fire department to have them

Arrangement of Candles

Shepherd 3 branch		Christ Candle		Wisemen 3 branch
○ ○ ○	Mary ○	○	Joseph ○	○ ○ ○

Altar

Paul
○

STEP

All Saints
○   ○   ○   ○

○
Bishop

○
Priest

○
Deacon

Apostles
○ ○ ○ ○ ○ ○   ○ ○ ○ ○ ○ ○
Apostles

Communion Rail

Church Militant
○

on hand. However, generally speaking, the fire chief will not recommend such a service. If you decide to have this service, be prepared and think ahead.

The candles and candle holders ought to be arranged so that the Christ Candle is highest. Hopefully the Christ Candle will be so high that a candlelighter will be necessary. The other acolytes may use candles.

Materials/People Needed for the Service of Light

People
    1 Liturgist
    1 Narrator
    1 Choir
    1 Soloist
    3 Kings (Soloists)
    2 Ushers
    9 Acolytes
    1 or 2 Light Technicians
    1 Director

Candles

1 Christ Candle	14 x 3''	
2 Altar Candles		
1 Candle	10 x 3''	Church Militant
26 Candles	9 x 7/8''	All other Candles
8 Candles	9 x 7/8''	For Acolytes
Congregation's Candles	6 7/8 x 17/32''	
Please provide drippers.		

Candle Holders
    1 Holder for the Christ Candle. This candle must be the highest candle in the chancel.
    2 Altar Candles. Use what is available — unless altar candles are unusually tall. For Mary and Joseph Candles.
    2 three branch candelabra

1 four branch candelabrum (Use a seven branch candelabrum and leave three holders empty.) 2 large floor candleholders. One for Paul and one for the Church Militant. These holders could be identical — but not necessary. (Note in the arrangement, Paul's candle must be taller than the Church Militant Candle. 12 glass star candle holders for the communion rail. 3 candleholders of equal size for Bishop, Priest, and Deacon. (I used 3 narrow crates, covered, and star candleholders.)

A Worship Bulletin Should be available for the Service.

THE SERVICE

Please remain seated during the Service; stand only for the Opening Hymn, for the Benediction, and the hymn, "A Mighty Fortress is Our God."

THE ORGAN PRELUDE

THE CONGREGATIONAL HYMN
"Christ Whose Glory Fills the Skies"

INTRODUCTION AND PRAYERS

NARRATOR: All people are seekers. On this Sunday following Epiphany, we recall the journeying of three Kings from the East, who followed a star from a far-off land to seek a promised gift. We remember not only them and their journey, but all those who have journeyed after them and have been witnesses to God shining forth in Jesus, the Light of the World. Let us pray.

PRAYERS FOR EPIPHANY
O God our Father, we often feel that we are living in shadows.
The shadows of bias . . .
The shadows of doubt . . .
The shadows of anxiety . . .
The shadows of limited information . . .
Help us to find your Light and to trust it. Help us to find your Light and share it. In Christ's name we pray. . . Amen.

Additional Prayers related to Epiphany might be used.

Our first lesson comes from the Book of Isaiah, telling of the coming of a Messiah.

FIRST LESSON: EXPECTATION   Isaiah 9:2-7
Liturgist: ". . . the jealous love of Yahweh Sabaoth will do this." [Pause]
Here ends the Lesson. [Liturgist sits down.]
Hymn: "Come Thou Long Expected Jesus"
                                        (Verses 1 and 2)
[Turn off all lights.]

THE CHRIST CANDLE

THE SECOND LESSON: John 1:1-5, 9-14   One Acolyte
Liturgist: ". . . full of grace and truth." [Pause]
Here ends the Lesson.
Solo: "O Holy Night"
[At the conclusion of the Solo, there is an organ bridge while one candlelighter enters to take his place at the altar. As the Narrator speaks, the Christ Candle is lighted. When the Narrator is finished the candlelighter sits down in the front row of the Sanctuary.]

Narrator:We light this candle, symbolizing Christ, the Light of the World.

MARY AND JOSEPH CANDLES

THE THIRD LESSON   Luke 2:1-7   One Acolyte
Liturgist: ". . . no place for them in the inn." [Pause]
Here ends the lesson. [Liturgist sits down.]
Hymn: "Silent Night"   (verse 1)
[During the singing of the hymn the candlelighters process into the Sanctuary and take their places at the side of the candles so they can light them while the Narrator is speaking. When the Narrator is finished, the candlelighters take their places in the front pew of the Sanctuary.]
Narrator: We light two candles . . . one for Mary and one for Joseph symbolizing the loving care they ministered to the son of man.

THE SHEPHERD CANDLES

THE FOURTH LESSON   Luke 2:8-20   One Acolyte
Liturgist: ". . . as it had been told them." [Pause]
Here ends the Lesson. [The Liturgist sits down.]
Hymn: "While Shepherds Watched Their Flocks"
                          (verse 1)
[During the singing of the hymn the acolyte processes into the Sanctuary taking his place in the Chancel, lights the candles while the Narrator is speaking, and then is seated.]
Narrator: We light candles representing the shepherds who abode in the fields around Bethlehem with their flocks, and who were the first to come to the Light.

THE WISE MEN CANDLES

THE FIFTH LESSON   Matthew 2:1-12   One Acolyte
Liturgist: ". . . they offered Him gifts: gold, and
frankincense and myrrh." [*Pause*]
   [*The liturgist sits down.*]
Hymn: "We Three Kings"   (five verses)
                Congregation sings refrain only.
[*The Three Kings sing the first verse from the rear of
the Sanctuary. Each solos as he processes to the
front of the Sanctuary to present his gift. Then the
three exit on the last verse.*]
Liturgist: "And being warned in a dream not to
return to Herod, they departed to their own country
by another way." [*Pause*]
   Here ends the Lesson. [*The liturgist sits down.*]
[*When the Liturgist sits down, the organist should
provide a bridge [Possibly "We Three Kings"] for
the acolyte to process into the Sanctuary. As the
Narrator is speaking the acolyte should light the
three candles and then be seated.*]
Narrator: We light three candles, one for each of
the Wise Men who were willing to look for the Light
in a strange land, and found it there.

THE APOSTLES' CANDLES

THE SIXTH LESSON   Matthew 10:1-4   Two Acolytes
[*The organist should provide a bridge for the
acolytes to enter the Sanctuary and assume their
places, before the Liturgist begins. The Liturgist must
wait for them to assume their positions. Then as the
Liturgist reads the names of the Apostles, the
acolytes light their candles. The Liturgist must watch
the acolytes to be certain that they can keep up with
him. If the acolytes begin at both ends of the
Communion Rail and work to the center, alternately
lighting candles, there should be no problem. When
all the candles are lighted the acolytes remain in
place.*]

Liturgist: ". . . and Judas Iscariot who betrayed
him." [*Pause*]
> Here ends the Lesson. [*The Liturgist is seated.*]
Hymn: "O Sacred Head Now Wounded" (Verse 1)
[*At the conclusion of the first verse of the hymn, one
candle, The Judas Candle, is extinguished. The
acolytes remain in place.*]

THE SEVENTH LESSON   Acts 1:15-26
Liturgist: ". . . And he was enrolled with the eleven
Apostles." [*Pause*]
> Here ends the Lesson. [*The Liturgist is seated.*]
Hymn: "O Sacred Head Now Wounded"
                              (Third Verse)
Narrator: The Light of Matthias now takes the place
of the traitor, Judas Iscariot.
Acolytes: [*The candle which was extinguished [the
Judas Candle] is relighted as the Narrator speaks.
The acolytes now leave the Communion Rail and
are seated.*]

THE ST. PAUL CANDLE

THE EIGHTH LESSON   Acts 9:1-8   One Acolyte
Liturgist: ". . . and brought him into Damascus."
[*Pause*]
> Here ends the Lesson.
Hymn: "I Love Thy Kingdom Lord" (Verses 1 and 4)
[*The acolyte should process during the hymn and
light his candle as the Narrator is reading. The
acolyte shall then be seated.*]
Narrator: We light a candle for Saul, who, to
symbolize his new-found life in Christ, changed his
name to Paul . . .

ALL SAINTS' CANDLES

THE NINTH LESSON   1 Corinthians 1:1-3   One Acolyte
Liturgist: ". . . God our Father and the Lord Jesus
Christ. [Pause]
    Here ends the Lesson.
Hymn: "For All the Saints"   (Verses 1 and 2)
[The acolyte should process during the hymn and
light the candles of the Saints as the names are read
by the Narrator.]
Narrator: We light candles for all the saints. But
herein especially, we remember:
    St. Mark, who was first to record Christ's life,
    death and resurrection;
    St. Matthew, who presents the teachings of the
    Church;
    St. Luke, gentle physician, who gave us the
    history of the early church,
    and St. John, the mystic, who explains the
    personhood of Christ.

THE CHURCH MILITANT

THE TENTH LESSON   Ephesians 6:10-20   One Acolyte
Liturgist: ". . . boldly, as I ought to speak." [Pause]
    Here ends the Lesson.
Hymn: "Jesus Shall Reign"   (Verses 1, 4, and 5)
[The acolyte will process during the hymn and be in
position to light the candles as the titles are read by
the Narrator. The Narrator must provide time for the
acolyte to move from candle to candle. The acolyte
then sits down.]
Narrator: We are the church militant, the transmitter
of the Light of the world to our generation and time.
We carry the GOOD NEWS to all, whether we are
bishops, priests, deacons, or laypersons. We are all
Christian people. And ours is the challenge to
enlighten our world where we are, that all men
might come to the Light and know the Life which is
his alone to give.

THE CHORAL ANTHEM
[*The ushers come forward, light their candles from the Church Militant candle [See diagram] and then light the candles of those persons seated along the center aisle. Each member then lights the candle of the person seated next to him and the light is passed throughout the church.*]
Liturgist: The Benediction   Ephesians 3:14-21
Hymn: "A Mighty Fortress is Our God"
[*As the hymn is being sung, the participants should leave the Sanctuary. The Narrator and Liturgist can join at the end of this processional. Then, the congregation exit singing. The effect is meant to be the church moving into the world. It is helpful if persons along the center aisle are advised ahead of time, so they can lead their pew from the Sanctuary. Furthermore, if it is desirable to carry lighted candles from the church, persons should wear their coats into the sanctuary or at least have them available.*]

—D. Gary Klempnauer

ADDITIONAL IDEAS
1. Make use of larger number of acolytes. In some churches the entire Junior High Youth Fellowship or Older Elementary Church School class could be used. Two acolytes could be used for the Joseph and Mary candles, four to light the candles of the saints, and twelve to light the apostles' candles.
2. Costumes can add to the effectiveness of this service. Provide colorful robes and head pieces for the three kings. All of the acolytes could be robed in white, or wear children's choir robes.
3. Continue the lighted procession (at the end of the service) into the outdoors. Process around the block, as a witness to the community, and back to the church sanctuary. Or, form a large star, in outline form, on the church lawn. Have everyone extinguish

their candles at a given signal.

4. Process into the social hall of the church for a period of fellowship. Have each person extinguish his candle as he enters the hall.

Noah and the Ark

Theme of the Service

The account of "Noah and the Flood" is no doubt one of the most popular Old Testament stories. It is so well known that we often fail to give full attention to what the story is saying to us. The purpose of this celebration is to present the old and familiar tale of Noah in a new and exciting manner. It is important, we feel, with such a familiar Scripture passage that congregational involvement in the unraveling of the story is necessary. To have someone say, "I took part in the flood," is more meaningful to that person than saying, "I heard the story of Noah and the flood."

Directions for the Service

When this celebration was originally presented in the Maplewood United Presbyterian Church of Greensburg, Pennsylvania, the congregation was divided into two equal parts facing one another. A table placed in the center made a natural division. These two groups shared in the liturgy by responding as the "right side" or "left side."

One person dressed in a robe plays the part of Noah. As the Scripture is read, Noah enacts the words. This enactment is all done at the table which divides the congregation and serves as the focal point for the sermon. Cut-outs of various animals have been passed out to children in the congregation. Noah calls each pair of animals, allowing time for the reader to give the statement about them. The children respond by bringing the animals to the ark and placing them inside.

The service concludes with a period of fellowship, in which coffee, doughnuts, and Kool-Aid are served.

With a few adaptations, this service can be presented successfully in a church sanctuary. Care should be taken, however, in giving specific instructions to all of the participants, especially the children who are to bring the animals forward at a specific time.

Materials Needed

1. Tape recorder.
2. Previously recorded tape
   a. "It's Rainin', I Believe," from the record, *Bible Songs and Stories*; Simon & Shuster, Inc. and Artists and Writers Guild, 630 Fifth Ave., New York, N.Y. 1957. (Side 1, band 4)
   b. Record of storm and rain.
3. Paper cut-outs of five pairs of animals — lions, eagles, camels, sheep and doves.
4. Altar, made in a metal container with stone or other base materials; small wood fire is formed in the center.
5. Robe for Noah.
6. Ark — to be constructed as desired.
7. Food — coffee, doughnuts, Kool-Aid, etc.
8. *Holy Bible*, Revised Standard Version.
   Ventures in Worship, David Randolph, editor; Abingdon Press, Nashville, Tenn., 1969.
9. Songs: "The Happy Side of Life" and "Let Us Break Bread Together" from *Reasons to Sing*, Lillenas Publishing Co., Kansas City, Mo. p. 9, 24. "Noah" from *Children's Liturgies*, Virginia Sloyan & Gabe Huck, ed.; Liturgical Conference, Washington, D.C., p.109. "Who Built the Ark?" from *Simple Songs for Toddlers*, Vol. III, Singspiration, Zondervan Publishing House, Grand Rapids, Mich. "Doxology" from *The Avery and Marsh Songbook*; Agape, Carol Stream, Ill., cover page. "The Lord's Prayer" from *A Time for Singing*; Geneva Press, Philadelphia, Pa., p. 13.
10. People: 10 children (to carry cut-outs of animals to ark and place them inside.)

THE SERVICE

PRELUDE — "It's Raining, It's Pouring"

THE SUMMONING [Read by right and left sides of congregation]

Right: We have come to this place as individuals; male and female have we come. We come from various backgrounds, interests, and locations.

Left: We too have come as individuals; male and female have we come. We come in different sizes, shapes, and colors.

Unison: We have all come because we are creatures. We have come to this place of worship because we are God's creatures.

Right: We've come, as did the animals to Noah, for we have been called by God's servant, Jesus.

Left: We've come in response to God's call to weather the storms of this life; to live and be fruitful and multiply.

Right: The voyage of this life will toss and turn us; it will make us comfortable and ill; it will dash us against the rocks of life.

Left: But the voyage will end, a rainbow will appear and the promises of God will give us hope for a better world.

Unison: Then let us celebrate our being God's creatures which have been granted safe passage through life.

HYMN   "Happy Side Of Life"

CONCERNS AND JOYS — [A time for those in the congregation to verbally mention those things which they wish to have included in prayer.]

SILENT PRAYER

CHORAL PRAYER OF INTERCESSION

Right: O Lord, we pray for the family and the home,
Left: And for those who are lonely and forgotten.
Right: We pray for our systems of law and order,
Left: And for those who suffer injustice.
Right: We pray for our varied religious forms,
Left: And for the divisions created by narrow-mindedness.
Right: We pray for our schools and colleges,
Left: And for those who are denied those benefits.
Right: We pray for our complex system of industry and business,
Left: And for those who are unable to find work.
Right: We pray for our institutions of international peace and understanding,
Left: And for those who are this day subjected to the pain and death of war.
Unison: In the name of Jesus, Amen. [*Ventures in Worship*]

PRAYER RESPONSE   "The Lord's Prayer"

ANNOUNCEMENTS

OFFERING   "Doxology"

HYMN   "Who Built the Ark?"

SERMON   "Noah's Ark"

READER: Following God's creation, there were many people on the face of the world. God was not pleased with these people for they had grown wicked. God was even sorry that he had created them and he was sad for having placed them on earth. So sad was God that he said, "I will destroy man and beast and the creeping things and the birds, for I am sorry I made them."

God looked over the face of the earth and found only one man who lived by his rules. His name was

Noah. [*Noah enters and approaches table.*] God looked kindly on Noah and said, "I intend to destroy the earth and everything on it. But, Noah, I want you to build an ark of gopher wood. [*Noah gathers materials to build the ark and begins working as the reader continues.*]

Make yourself an ark of gopher wood; make rooms in the ark, and cover it inside and out with pitch. This is how you are to make it: the length of the ark three hundred cubits, its breadth fifty cubits, and its height thirty cubits. Make a roof for the ark and finish it to a cubit above; and set the door of the ark in its side; make it with lower, second, and third decks. [*Noah builds the ark.*]

But I will establish my covenant with you; and you shall come into the ark, you, your sons, your wife, and your sons' wives with you. And of every living thing of all flesh, you shall bring two of every sort into the ark, to keep them alive with you; they shall be male and female. Of the birds according to their kinds, and of the animals according to their kinds, of every creeping thing of the ground according to its kind, two of every sort shall come in to you, to keep them alive." [*There are five pairs of animals. Noah calls each, giving time for reader to make statement about these animals. Children bring animals to the ark and place them in the ark.*]

NOAH: Let the lions come forward.

READER: The Scriptures tell us the lion, the king of the animal kingdom, will one day lie down with the lamb. The ferociousness of the lion will unite with the gentleness of the lamb.

NOAH: Let the eagles come.

READER: The people of God will one day rise up with the wings of eagles and the kingdom will prosper.

NOAH: Let the camels walk on board.

READER: Jesus said it was easier for this large burdensome animal to pass through the eye of a needle than for a rich man to enter the kingdom of God.

NOAH: The sheep will come on board.

READER: The day of judgment will find the sheep going with the Father, and the goats into eternal damnation.

NOAH: Let the doves fly to me.

READER: The dove is the symbol of peace.

[*The tape is turned on with the song "It's Rainin', I Believe", Bible Songs and Stories.*]

The Lord told Noah he had a plan,
To punish the evil come to man.
Flood the earth and clean the land.
The world is gonna grieve.
Noah brought his family near.
He said, "The sky don't look so clear.
Get the animals, bring 'em here,
It's rainin', I believe."

CHORUS:

Children, little children,
The ark is gonna leave,
So step inside and take a ride.
It's rainin', I believe.

Noah built himself an ark.
Built it from the hickory bark.
All the world was gettin' dark.
The boat's about to leave.
Animals come in one by one,
Cow a-chewin' a carroway bun.
Milk she carried weighed a ton.
It's rainin', I believe.

Animals come in two by two,
Rhinoceros and the kangaroo,
Gorilla wore one brand new shoe,

The boat's about to leave.
Animals come in three by three,
The bear a-huggin' a bumbly bee,
Hyena laughed and slapped his knee,
It's rainin', I believe.

Animals come in four by four,
Noah he said, "there's room for more."
The flea hollered out, "Don't close that door!"
The boat's about to leave.
Animals come in five by five,
From all the lands they did arrive,
Tickled to death to be alive,
It's rainin', I believe.
CHORUS
Animals come in six by six,
Hyena laughed at the monkey's tricks,
Skunk was too polite to mix,
The boat's about to leave.
Animals come in seven by seven,
The big and the little ones under heaven,
Said the ant to the elephant, "Quit your shovin,"
It's rainin', I believe.

Animals come in eight by eight,
The armadilla he found a mate,
Noah hollered, "Go shut that gate!"
The boat's about to leave.
Animals come in nine by nine,
Last one in was a porcupine,
Noah hollered, "Go cut that line!"
It's rainin', I believe.
The ark moved out on the mornin' tide,
Travelled the world both far and wide,
Whale he took his pretty bride,
The boat's about to leave.
    [*Here the song fades away and a simulated rain
storm is heard. The lights in the room are turned out*

and as the storm continues, the reader says . . .]

READER: The heavens opened and the rain fell. For forty days and forty nights it rained, until the mountains of earth were covered with water.

[*The storm continues and then subsides with the last stanza of "It's Rainin', I Believe" being sung and the lights come on.*]

Noah sent out the mornin' dove,
To find a leaf on the land above,
The dove came back on the wings of love,
He found it, I believe.

CHORUS

Children, little children,
Now, don't you fret and grieve,
They ended up at Mount Ararat,
And it has stopped
It's rainin', I believe!

READER: At the end of forty days Noah opened the window of the ark which he had made, and sent forth a raven; and it went to and fro until the waters were dried up from the earth. Then he sent forth a dove from him, to see if the waters had subsided from the face of the ground; and the dove came back to him in the evening, and lo, in her mouth a freshly plucked olive leaf; so Noah knew that the waters had subsided from the earth.

Then God said to Noah, "Go forth from the ark, you and your wife, and your sons and your sons' wives with you. Bring forth with you every living thing that is with you of all flesh — birds and animals and every creeping thing that creeps on the earth — that they may breed abundantly on the earth, and be fruitful and multiply upon the earth." So Noah went forth, and his sons and his wife and his sons' wives with him. And every beast, every creeping thing, and every bird everything that moves upon the earth, went forth by families out of the ark.

[Noah leaves the ark, taking the cut-out animals and food with him. A small altar has been erected in sight of everyone; the cut-outs are placed on the altar and burned.]

READER: Then Noah built an altar to the Lord, and took of every clean animal and of every clean bird, and offered burnt offerings on the altar. And when the Lord smelled the pleasing odor, the Lord said in his heart, "I will never again curse the ground because of man, for the imagination of man's heart is evil from his youth; neither will I ever again destroy every living creature as I have done.

And God said, This is the sign of the covenant which I make between me and you and every living creature that is with you, for all future generations: I set my bow in the clouds, and it shall be a sign of the covenant between me and the earth.

HYMN   "Let Us Break Bread Together"

BENEDICTION:
NOAH: "Go into the world and multiply."

FELLOWSHIP OF COFFEE AND DOUGHNUTS
— I. Lee Page
— Nancy C. Burke

ADDITIONAL IDEAS
1. Service could easily be adapted to use of puppets.
2. Vacation Church School would be an ideal place to use this service. It could be presented by an older elementary or junior high group for the benefit of all the children.
3. Consider introducing audio-visuals, especially slides, and expanding the service into a longer program. Make your own slides or take slides of children which would portray and expand the Noah story.

4. Give consideration to serializing the story into several segments — children and adults relate well to this technique. This would be especially desirable if slides or puppets were used.

5. Use this as an outdoor service, perhaps with a few live animals. Consider using it as worship service for a church picnic or at a weekend family camp, in months when the weather would permit.

The Meal in the Upper Room

Theme of the Service

This service is a commemorative meal and inspirational experience which can be used effectively in preparation for Holy Week in the church. Those who participate in the eating of the meal are bound together in fellowship as they share the common meal in commemoration of the Last Supper which Jesus ate with his friends. It was the occasion during which Jesus laid upon their hearts his parting messages. These final messages are repeated in this service, in the reading of his own words from the Scriptures:

The lighting of the Passover candles and the reading of the Passover Thanksgiving are features of this meal in every Jewish home. Here it becomes a family service in which all members participate. Passages of the ancient Hebrew "Hallel" (Psalms 113 and 114) were no doubt repeated by Jesus and his disciples, and they are used in this service to heighten the memory of the original occasion.

The participants should not think of this meal as the institutionalized communion service of the early church, but should instead try to recapture the spirit of the admonitions Jesus gave his disciples during their last meal together.

Directions for the Service

The members of the congregation should assemble promptly (such as at 6:30 p.m. on the Monday before Easter) in a designated room of the church where coats and hats are left. Let them then proceed in silence to the sanctuary for the "preparation."

An organ prelude of pastoral Hebrew themes is most appropriate. After the service of preparation concluding with the hymn, "Beneath the Forms of Outward Rite," have the congregation proceed silently to the dining room where only candles required to show the way are lighted.

The tables may be placed in the form of a square, with a smaller square within the larger one if necessary. It is preferable to seat all the people facing the center. Each place should have the following: a plain white mat, a soft white napkin, and a galax leaf on which the thinly-sliced lamb and endive are placed. There should be a paper cup for the grapejuice. Other foods can be arranged attractively in these positions:

grapes			parsley	cup
			green olive	
orange			ripe olive	
		cheese		
napkin			lamb and	
			endive on	
	pecans		leaf	
dates				matzos

Make "candleboards" to hold seven candles for each table. These will supplement the single candles and the seven branch candelabrum. Use the previously lighted single candles to light the seven candle arrangements during the meal. Huckleberry or other leaves can be used around the candle holders.

The music suggested is that which was used when this service was held at Wesley United Methodist Church in Mason City, Iowa. Feel free to use other appropriate music. Use no music that contains the word "cross" as they did not know of the crucifixion at the Last Supper. The oboe, flute, or piccolo are effective, as are the harp or any old-fashioned stringed instrument (such as a zither), since they add to the pastoral atmosphere. Hine Mah Tov (three melodies), which means "Behold how good and pleasant it is for brethren to dwell in unity," is suitable for the above instruments.

The first century atmosphere is enhanced by the use of brass, pewter, and copper pitchers for the grape juice; metal or wood trays for the fruit; and woven baskets for the matzos.

It is important to prepare the congregation for this experience long before it takes place. In Wesley Church, a Lenten folder was mailed several weeks in advance; an explanation of the service was given and reservations were requested. In this case, the meal was limited to 100 persons and each was asked to contribute to cover the cost of the food.

Part of the success of the service at Wesley Church was due to the large number of persons involved in it. Instead of having one person read the Scripture passages, these were presented by six different young people. Different persons were also used to present the musical selections in the form of solos and trios; there were others who presented selections on the instruments named above. Of course, many persons were involved in preparing and serving the commemorative meal.

Materials/People Needed
1. Pastor as leader.
2. Vocalists for solo and trio numbers.
3. Six youth readers.
4. Father(blesses the meal)
5. Mother (prayer — lighting Passover candles)
6. Hymns: "Dear Lord and Father of Mankind"
              "Beneath the Forms of Outward Rite"
              "O Master, Let Me Walk With Thee"
7. Vocal Selections:
       "God So Loved the World" — Stainer
       "Peace I Leave With You" — Roberts
       "I Heard the Voice of Jesus Say" — Dykes
       "This is My Commandment" — Hamblen
8. Candelabra and candle holders of brass and wood.
9. Food for the Passover Meal:
       (Recipe serves 250 persons)
       6 legs of lamb (boned and sliced)
       28 lbs. of red Tokay grapes
       16 pkgs. fresh dates (not pitted)

2 bunches parsley
3 bunches endive
14 doz. Temple or navel oranges
3 qts. green olives (not pitted)
6 large cans ripe olives (medium size)
34 qts. grape juice
10 lbs. medium sharp cheese
3 lbs. shelled pecans
1 doz. boxes matzos

[*Have butcher bone and tie lamb. Cook it and return to him to be refrigerated and then sliced. Separate grapes into small bunches of six or eight grapes. Peel oranges and quarter. Give each person two or three quarters. Dilute grape juice, 3 grape juice diluted with 2 bottles of water will serve twelve to fourteen persons. Cut cheese into small cubes.*

THE SERVICE

PRELUDE

INTRODUCTORY THOUGHTS CONCERNING THE PASCHAL MEAL [Pastor]

In the East, a meal has a peculiar significance which it does not have for us of the West. In the East, eating together is in itself a pledge of friendship and loyalty. In the eating of this meal we are binding ourselves in fellowship by sharing together the common meal in commemoration of the Last Supper which Jesus ate with his friends. Will you not be thinking of this meal as an expression in itself of your love and loyalty to Jesus?

We can imagine that Peter and John have made the preparations, provided the food out of the common treasury, and set the table for guests. Tonight as in that upper room we will be served roast lamb, matzos (unleavened bread), bitter herbs (endive), Passover wine (grape juice), ripe and green olives, dates, figs, nuts, cheese, and grapes. It was an intimate occasion. All were filled with the same sense of impending events, momentous in character, for each of them and for the group. It was an occasion in which Jesus, closer to his followers than ever before, laid upon their hearts his parting messages and instructions. In loving remembrance, these final messages will be repeated in the reading of his own words. Passages of the ancient Hebrew "Hallel" (Psalms 113 and 114), repeated no doubt by Jesus and his disciples, will be read to heighten the memory of the original occasion.

The lighting of the Passover candles and the reading of the Passover Thanksgiving were features of this meal in every Jewish home. We are trying to think of this meal not as the intitutionalized Communion Service of the early church but are trying to recapture the spirit of the admonitions Jesus gave his disciples during their last meal together.

The meal is to be eaten during the service. Serve yourself generously and pass to others. There is plenty of food for a satisfying meal, although the food is secondary to the spiritual implications of communion. Silence is to be maintained until leaving the church.

THE PRAYER [in unison]

Almighty God, Father of Abraham, Isaac, and Jacob, and Father of our Lord Jesus Christ: Be with us this night as we enter with the disciples of old a room prepared for us. Help us to discover in our celebration of the Passover Meal the deep meaning placed there by Jesus. Let it be a time of fellowship, for we are brothers and sisters in Christ, and a time of a deepening relationship with you, the Creator of us all. We ask these things in the name of him who calls us to this meal, even Jesus Christ our Lord and Savior. Amen.

THE PREPARATION FOR THE MEAL
    The Invitation   Luke 14:12-16
    The Preparation   Luke 22:1-13

THE HYMN   "Beneath the Forms of Outward Rite"
1. Beneath the forms of outward rite,
   Thy Supper, Lord is spread,
   In every quiet upper room
   Where fainting souls are fed.
2. The bread is always consecrate,
   Which men divide with men;
   And every act of brotherhood,
   Repeats the feast again.
3. The blessed cup is only passed
   True memory of thee,
   When life anew pours out its wine,
   With rich sufficiency.
4. O Master, through these symbols shared,
   Thine own dear self impart,
   That in our daily life may flame
   The passion of thy heart. Amen.

[Congregation proceeds to "Upper Room" in silence]

THE PASSOVER MEAL

I. THE LIGHTING OF THE PASSOVER CANDLES

PRAYER (By a mother)
    Blessed art Thou, O Lord our God, King of the universe, who has sanctified us by thy Commandments and commanded us to kindle the festival lights. Blessed art Thou, O Lord our God, King of the universe, who has kept us alive and

sustained us and brought us to this season. May our home be consecrated, O God, by the light of thy countenance, shining upon us in blessing and bringing us to peace. Amen.
[*Have the guests to the right of the candelabra use the tapers to light them at this time.*]

II. THE KIDDUSH, BLESSING OF THE FEAST

PRAYER OF BLESSING [*By a father*]
Blessed art Thou, O Lord, our God, King of the universe, who hast chosen us above all people, and hast exalted us above all tongues, and hast hallowed us with thy commandments. In love hast Thou given us, O Lord our God, seasons of gladness, holy-days, and times for rejoicing this day of the feast of the unleavened bread, the time of our freedom, an assembly-day of holiness, a memorial to the exodus from Egypt. For Thou hast chosen us and hast sanctified us above all peoples, and Thou hast given us Thy sacred seasons for our inheritance. Blessed art Thou, O Lord, who dost sanctify Israel and the festivals. Amen.

THE SHARING OF THE CUP
All: Blessed art Thou, O Lord our God, King of the universe, who dost create the fruit of the vine.
[*Sip from the cup of juice*]

THE SHARING OF THE BITTER HERBS
All: Blessed art Thou, O Lord our God, King of the universe, who dost create the fruit of the soil.
[*Dip herbs in salt water*]

III. THE HAGGADAH
[*Story of the deliverance from Egypt*]

THE QUESTIONS: [*Asked by girls*]
Why is this night different from all other nights? On all other nights we eat either leavened or unleavened bread. Why on this night do we eat only unleavened bread?

THE QUESTIONS: [*Asked by boys*]
On all other nights we eat all kinds of herbs. Why on this night do we eat especially bitter herbs? On all other nights we do not dip herbs. Why on this night do we dip them in salt water? On all other nights we eat without special festivities. Why on this night do we hold this passover service?

THE STORY OF DELIVERANCE   Exodus 12
[*As the leader lifts the paschal lamb, all will ask:*]
What is the meaning of Pesach? [*Pronounced pea-sock*]
[*As the leader lifts the unleavened bread and holds it up, all will ask:*]
What is the meaning of Matzo?
[*As the leader lifts up the bitter herbs, all will ask:*]
What is the meaning of Moror? [*Pronounced mor-ror*]

IV. *THE PRAYER OF THANKSGIVING*
(From Psalms 113 and 114)
Pastor: Please stand and recite before God a new song.
People: Hallelujah, praise the Lord!
Pastor: When Israel went out of Egypt, the house of Jacob from a barbarous people:
People: Judea was made his sanctuary, Israel his dominion.
Pastor: The sea was quickly broken apart before them and the Jordan turned back.
People: The mountains skipped like rams, and the hills like the lambs of the flock.

Pastor: What ailed thee, O sea, that thou didst flee; and thou, O Jordan, that thou wast turned back?

People: Ye mountains, that ye skipped like rams, and ye hills, like lambs of the flock?

Pastor: At the presence of the Lord the earth was moved, at the presence of the God of Jacob.

People: He it was who turned the rock into pools of water, and the stony hill into fountains of waters. Hallelujah, praise the Lord!

V. THE SOLEMN BLESSING OF THE FOOD

Pastor: Blessed art thou, O Lord, who dost redeem Israel.

People: Blessed art thou, O Lord our God, King of the universe, who dost create the fruit of the vine.

[All take another drink from their cup.]

Pastor: Blessed art thou, O Lord our God, King of the universe, who dost bring forth bread from the earth.

People: Blessed art thou, O Lord our God, King of the universe, who hast sanctified us by thy commandments and hast commanded us concerning the eating of the unleavened bread.

Pastor: Let us combine the unleavened bread and the bitter herbs and eat them together, as it is written: "With unleavened bread and with bitter herbs, they shall eat it."

People: Blessed art thou, O Lord our God, King of the universe, who has sanctified us by thy commandments and hast commanded us concerning the eating of bitter herbs.

VI. THE PASCHAL SUPPER TAKES PLACE

[The people will begin eating, but retain a portion of the unleavened bread and the grape juice for the formal Breaking of the Bread. They will eat in silence while the Scriptures are read and vocal selections are presented.]

THE TRIO   "God So Loved the World"   Stainer

THE SCRIPTURE [1st reader]
The Law of the Kingdom Luke 13:18-21   Luke 17:20-21
                      Luke 22:28-30   John 13:13-18
The True Treasure   Luke 12:15-32

THE TRIO   "Peace I Leave With You"   Roberts

THE SCRIPTURE [2nd reader]
    Desire to Eat Passover With You   Luke 22:15-16
    Intimate Personal Messages, Admonitions and
        Charges:
    A. John 13:33   **John 14:6-7**   B. John14:18-29
       John 14:1-4   **John 14:10-17**

THE SOLO   "I Heard the Voice of Jesus Say"   Dykes

THE SCRIPTURE [3rd reader]
    Personal Message [Cont'd]   John 15:1-16
    Admonitions of Jesus **John 15:17-27**   John 16:1-7
                             John 16:19-28

THE SOLO   "This Is My Commandment"   Hamblen

THE SCRIPTURE [4th reader]
    The Meditation   Luke 22:31-32
    The Farewell Message   John 16:32-33

THE SCRIPTURE [The pastor]
    The Farewell Prayer   John 17:1-11, 16-17, 20-26

THE LORD'S PRAYER [In unison]

THE HYMN   "Dear Lord and Father of Mankind"

THE SCRIPTURE [5th reader]
    The New Covenant   Matthew 5:17,21-22,
                             27-28, 38-48

THE SCRIPTURE [*The pastor*]
The Breaking of Bread   1 Corinthians 5:8
Luke 22:19-20
The Prayer   John 17:18-26
[*The people may partake of the remainder of the bread and the juice here. If it is desired to have the Holy Communion later, this section may be omitted.*]

THE SCRIPTURE [*6th reader*]
A New Commandment   John 13:31-35

THE HYMN   "O Master Let Me Walk With Thee"
[*Use if service is concluded here followed by Holy Communion. If so, let the people leave quietly humming the hymn. If Communion does not follow omit the hymn and continue as follows.*

VII. *THE BREAKING OF THE BREAD — THE CUP OF BLESSING*
Pastor: Let us bless the Lord.
People: May the name of the Lord be blessed from now unto eternity.
Pastor: Blessed art thou, O Lord our God, King of the universe, who dost feed the entire world with thy goodness, with grace, with loving kindness and with pity. He gives bread to all flesh, for his loving kindness endures forever. And in his great goodness, food has been given for us all forever and ever. He feeds and supports all, and does good untc all, and prepares food for all his creatures which he did create.
People: Blessed art thou, O Lord, who gives freedom to all thy creatures.
Pastor: What shall I render to the Lord for all the things he has rendered to me?

People: I will take the chalice of salvation and I will call upon the name of the Lord.

Pastor: I will pay my vows to the Lord before all his people.

People: Precious in the sight of the Lord is the death of his saints.

Pastor: I will pay my vows to the Lord in the sight of all his people, in the courts of the house of the Lord, in the midst of thee, O Jerusalem.

People: Blessed art thou, O Lord our God, King of the universe, who has created the fruit of the vine.

Pastor: Holy art thou, Almighty and Merciful God. Holy art thou, and great is the majesty of thy glory. Thou didst so love the world as to give thine only begotten Son, that whosoever believeth in him might not perish, but have everlasting life: who, having come into the world to fulfill for us thy holy will and to accomplish all things for our salvation, in the night when he was betrayed, took bread; and when he had given thanks, he broke it and gave it to his disciples saying, "Take and eat, this is my body, which is given for you. This do in remebrance of me."

[*All shall eat the matzo.*]

Pastor: After the supper in the same manner also, he took the cup, when he had supped, and when he had given thanks, he gave it to them, saying, "Drink ye all of it. This cup is the New Testament in my blood, which is shed for you, and for many, for the remission of sins. This do, as oft as ye shall drink of it, in remembrance of me."

[*All shall drink the juice.*]

THE LORD'S PRAYER

THE BLESSING [*In unison*]   Numbers 6:24-26
   May the Lord bless and protect you; may the
Lord's face radiate with joy because of you; may he
be gracious to you, show you his favor, and give
you his peace. Amen.

THE HYMN   "O Master Let Me Walk With Thee"
[*Let the people leave quietly, humming the hymn.*]
                   —Keith L. Scott

ADDITIONAL IDEAS
1. This service may be used in several forms. It may
   end with Section VI. Or, the last part of Section VI
   (from the Breaking of Bread Scripture) may be
   omitted and the service concluded with Section VII.
2. Section VI may be condensed, omitting all music,
   merely reading the Scripture passages.
3. Sections III, IV, and V may be omitted, with Section
   VI being followed in its complete form.
4. This service in its complete form is quite lengthy. If
   you are presenting it to your congregation for the
   first time, it is suggested that you use a condensed
   form. Then, use an expanded version of it the
   following year when your people are more familiar
   with it.

Celebrating Easter

Theme of the Service

This service, planned for a United Church of Christ in Texas, is designed to present the true meaning of Easter — not just through liturgy and sermon, but also through the presentation of a family experience. As each member of the family presents what Easter means to him, the theme moves from a secular to a spiritual emphasis. Most children, as well as adults, will follow this progression — to their level of understanding.

Directions for the Service

This should be a dignified service of worship, and it is important that the family sharing experience be well rehearsed. Not to do so could create a slip-shod atmosphere that would limit the effectiveness of the service. It may be adapted to the local situation and the family presenting it. This family should be carefully selected so that it will be well done. In some cases, it will be presented most effectively by four persons who are not members of the same family.

The symbols referred to in the sharing time should be visible to all. If they are not to be found in the paraments, or stained glass windows, some large symbols may be made from cardboard or styrofoam and prominently displayed. A book on Christian symbols should be secured from your bookstore, or library, for further elaboration on Easter symbols and their meaning.

Materials/People Needed
1. Basket with Easter eggs (1st child)
2. Bible (1st parent)
3. Family Sharing Participants:
   Small child
   Older child
   First parent

Second parent
4. Easter symbols:
   Lamb of God
   Easter lilies
   Cross
   Butterfly
5. Hymns:
   "Christ the Lord is Risen Today"
   "Come, Ye Faithful, Raise the Strain"
   "Jesus Christ is Risen Today"
   "Jesus Lives and So Shall I"
   "The Strife is O'er"
   "Thine is the Glory"
   "The Day of Ressurection"
   "Welcome, Happy Morning"
6. Choral Anthem

THE SERVICE

PRAYER BEFORE THE SERVICE [*To be read silently*]
O God of peace: Fill our hearts with faith, that with joy and thanksgiving we may remember his triumph over death. Inspire us in all our efforts to praise you, in the name of him who brought newness of life, even Jesus Christ our Lord. Amen.

PRELUDE

OPENING SENTENCES
Pastor: He has risen. (Mark 16:6)
People: He has risen indeed. (Luke 24:34)
Pastor: Death is swallowed up in victory. (1 Corinthians 15:54)
People: Christ being raised from the dead will never die again; death no longer has dominion over him. He died to sin, once for all, but the life he lives he lives to God. (Romans 6:9-10)

Pastor: Therefore, let us keep the feast, not with old leaven, neither with leaven of malice and wickedness, but with the unleavened bread of sincerity and truth. (1 Corinthians 5:7,8)

People: Thanks be to God, who gives us the victory through our Lord Jesus Christ. [1 Corinthians 15:57)

PROCESSIONAL HYMN   "Christ the Lord is Risen Today"

CONFESSION OF SIN

Pastor: If we confess our sins, God is faithful and just, and will forgive our sins and cleanse us from all unrighteousness. Let us confess our sins to Almighty God.

Pastor and People: Gracious God, Father of our Lord Jesus Christ: You have promised to receive us when we come to you. We confess that we have sinned against you in thought, word and deed. We have disobeyed your law. We have not loved you or our neighbors as we should. Forgive us, O God, and grant that we may live and serve you in newness of life, through Jesus Christ our Lord. Amen.1

KYRIE ELEISON [*May be said or sung*]

Pastor: Lord, have mercy on us.
People: Lord, have mercy on us.
Pastor: Christ, have mercy on us.
People: Christ, have mercy on us.
Pastor: Lord, have mercy on us.
People: Lord, have mercy on us.

ASSURANCE OF PARDON

Pastor: Beloved, God has promised us mercy and has given us his Son, Jesus Christ, to die for our sins that we may live in newness of life, obedient to his will. Therefore, I announce, in the name of Christ, that your sins are forgiven, according to the promises in the Gospel. Amen.[1]

ASCRIPTION OF PRAISE
Pastor: O Lord, open our lips.
People: And our mouths shall show forth your praise.

HYMN   "The Strife is O'er" or
"Come, Ye Faithful, Raise the Strain"

A FAMILY SHARES IN THE MEANING OF EASTER
1st Child: I can remember the Easter egg hunt, when we went out with a basket and found Easter eggs — pink, yellow and blue eggs. We never thought about how hard it would be for the Easter bunny to bring the eggs to our home for us all to enjoy. It was fun and we knew that Easter was an important day! [*A basket of eggs may be carried and eggs shown.*]

2nd Child: Weeks before Easter we began to think of the clothes we would wear. We were excited, even though we knew that Easter was more than a time for new clothes. We were dressing for the most important day of the Church year and we were getting ready to join many others in singing, praying, listening, rejoicing, and hoping for the blessings God had in store for us!

1st Parent: We have been emphasizing in many of our families, and in our Church School and Church Services that Easter is more than a celebration of the renewal of nature in the springtime — more than expressions of beauty and the newest clothes we could put on. Easter means that long ago Jesus arose, after being crucified, dead and buried.

2nd Parent: And even more than that — Easter means that because he lives, we too shall live!

1st Parent: Years ago our pastor explained some Easter symbols to us. I hope I can recall what he said. The Lamb of God, crucified for our sins, was now risen. We are reminded of that by the embroidery on the pulpit hanging [Or elsewhere] where the lamb is standing and carrying a resurrection banner. Easter lilies bloom around Easter, and are sometimes pictured around the cross. The cross is empty; Christ was taken from the cross and it stands in its beauty for the love of God shown in Jesus Christ, who reigns for all eternity, that we might have newness of life. The windows in our church sanctuary speak artistically of this revelation — centering in the crucifixion, the resurrection, and ascension of our Lord. The butterfly, with its new body, is symbolic of the change that will take place, since the mourning cloak butterfly hatches from the egg as a tiny caterpillar, then mysteriously emerges in all its beauty as a butterfly reminding us of what St. Paul says in the Scriptures:

". . .. is not the spiritual which is first but the physical, and then the spiritual. The first man was from earth, a man of dust; the second is from heaven. As was the man of dust, so are those who are of the dust; and as is the man of heaven, so are those who are of heaven. Just as we have borne the image of the man of dust, we shall also bear the image of the man of heaven." (1 Corinthians 15:46-49)

PRAYER [By one of the parents]
O merciful and all-powerful God, who raised Jesus Christ from the dead, we invoke your presence and inspiration, beseeching you to renew our inner life that we may seek those things which are above. Send ministering spirits to roll away the stones from our

hearts, that we may believe, even if we haven't seen. Help us to walk by faith as well as by sight, to trust and not be afraid. Equip us with everything good, working in us that which is pleasing in your sight, through Jesus Christ, to whom with you and the Holy Spirit be glory for ever and ever. Amen. [2]

ANTHEM

EASTER COLLECT

Risen and victorious Christ, surprise us with joy as you surprised the visitors at your tomb on that first Easter morning, that we may experience your glorious resurrection and be worthy instruments of your love and power for the glory of your name and the advancement of your ministry. Amen. [3]

SCRIPTURE READINGS

The First Lesson: Acts 10:34-43
The Second Lesson: Colossians 3:1-11
The Gospel: John 20:1-9

HYMN   "The Day of Resurrection"

SERMON

AFFIRMATION OF FAITH

ANTHEM   "Welcome, Happy Morning"

HYMN   "Jesus Christ is Risen Today"

PRAYERS

Pastor: The Lord be with you.
People: And with you also.

Pastor: Let us Pray
[*Prayers of thanksgiving, praise, and intercession will follow.*]

OFFERING
Offertory Sentence (Matthew 6:19-21)
Presentation of Tithes and Offerings
Offertory Selection
Doxology and Prayer of Dedication

SACRAMENT OF HOLY COMMUNION [*Optional*]

HYMN   "Thine is the Glory" or
                    "Jesus Lives and So Shall I"

COMMISSION
      Go forth into the world in peace; be of good
courage; hold fast to that which is good; render to
no one evil for evil; strengthen the fainthearted;
support the weak; help the afflicted; honor all
people; love and serve the Lord; rejoice in the
power of the Holy Spirit.[1]

BLESSING
      The grace of our Lord Jesus Christ, the love of
God, and the communion of the Holy Spirit, be with
you all. Amen. (2 Corinthians 13:14)

POSTLUDE

—Friedrich Rest

1. From SERVICE OF WORD AND SACRAMENT I by the
   Commission on Worship, United Church of Christ,
   as printed in *The Hymnal of the United Church of
   Christ*, United Church Press, Philadelphia, 1974.
2. Rest, Friedrich, *Our Christian Worship: Resources for
   Palm Sunday Through Easter*, C.S.S. Publishing Co.,
   Lima, Ohio 1977.

3. Adapted from *Book of Worship,* General Synod of the Evangelical and Reformed Church, Central Publishing House, Cleveland, Ohio 1947.

ADDITIONAL IDEAS

1. Allow children to leave sanctuary during sermon and serving of Holy Communion. Have them go to a Church School classroom to make some of the Easter symbols of cardboard, or paint them on large sheets of paper. These can be displayed for the congregation to view as they leave the sanctuary.
2. Have all of the children in the congregation come to the chancel for the explanation of the symbols. Otherwise, they may be unable to see them and fail to understand the symbolism.
3. Create large mobiles using Christian symbols and hang them about the church — but outside the sanctuary.
4. Make several large cloth banners (4 feet by 8 feet or 12 feet) of bright colors utilizing simple imagery symbols of the resurrection. Hang these banners outside the church building, over the primary entrance to the church. The banners would need to be in scale to the building.
5. Create audio-visual centers outside the sanctuary. Using slides, portray persons creating the symbols, banners, etc., preparing for the Easter service. Photographs could be displayed in these areas, as well as art work from the Church School.

Honoring Grandmothers

Theme of the Service

This service is a liturgy geared to and involving children. It contains the elements of worship (the prayers, the Scripture, the proclaiming of the Word) but these are slanted to speak to children.

A children's liturgy does not deal with deep theological questions but attempts to celebrate a specific and concrete theme. In this one, which was used in a United Methodist Church in Virginia, we celebrate grandmothers. Hopefully, by celebrating grandmothers, the children will be given a sense of roots and security and see the on-going debt we owe past generations in the passing on of our faith.

There are several ways in which children's liturgies are different. Children respond more to color. Thus, in the opening procession a colorful paper chain, made by the children, is brought in and placed on the altar. This also serves as a focal point for them during the service, symbolizing the chain of faith through the years.

Children must move; thus, this service may have more ups and downs than you normally experience. Their interest span is short, so there is no lengthy sermon. Instead, there is a time of "sharing memories" by grandmothers and, if desired, a short meditation by the minister.

Music is also an important part of a children's liturgy. Since children love to repeat a song, the opening and closing hymn in this service are the same.

Directions for the Service

There are several very important things to consider in your plannng and preparation for this service.

1. Encourage the children of your congregation to bring their grandmothers to the service. If you live near a nursing or retirement home, a very meaningful

experience can result from "adopting" a grandmother for the day.

2. Contact some of the grandmothers before the service and encourage them to share memories. Emphasize that they must be brief; it will be better to have a number of short memories than to allow one person to monopolize this important period of the service.

3. Have the children in your Church School make a simple paper chain by stapling together colorful strips of construction paper. Practice processing into the sanctuary with this chain at least once. Strive for a sense of reverence and dignity.

4. Discuss the service with the minister, or leader, beforehand. This should be a person who is able to evoke participation from the congregation. This is a necessary part of both the opening section and the time of prayer.

Materials/People Needed
1. Paper chain (made from colored construction paper).
2. Grandmothers (lots of them)!
3. Adult reader (for two readings if not given by minister).
4. Child reader (for reading New Testament Scripture).
5. Hymns and songs:
   "Faith of our Fathers — Hymnal
   "Happy the Home When God is There — Hymnal
   "Pass it On" — *Hymns for Now III,* Vol. 4, No. 1
Concordia Publishing House, St. Louis, Missouri.

OPENING HYMN   "Faith of Our Fathers"
[During the singing, the children process down aisle
with long paper chain and place it on the altar.]

GREETING
Minister: Welcome to our children's liturgy!
Today we come together for a very special
purpose. We come to celebrate our grandmothers. The Chinese have a saying, "The home
which has an old grandparent in it contains a
precious jewel." Many of you have your grandparents with you today. Some have "adopted"
grandparents for the day. We would like to take
a few minutes to welcome these special guests
to our service. Will all of our grandparents
please stand? Now, will each child share with us
where your grandparent is from? [Allow
sufficient time for introductions.]

RESPONSIVE SENTENCES
Minister: Let's all join now in these opening
sentences: For the love of our grandparents —
People: We give you thanks.
Minister: For the homes that nurture and shelter
us —
People: We give you thanks.
Minister: For our Christian faith which has been
passed down through loving generations —
People: We give you thanks.

PASSING THE FAITH
Minister: The long chain made by the children
of the Church School and placed on our altar
today is a reminder to us of the way our
Christian faith has been passed down through the
ages — a long chain of faith. If no one had told
you about Jesus and our history as a people
whose roots are in the Scriptures, how would

you have known? How fortunate is the child who grows up in a home aware of our Christian heritage.

Let me explain to you in another way how this works. Will everyone please stand and join hands? Now, will the person standing nearest the aisle squeeze the hand he is holding. As soon as that person feels the squeeze he will pass it on to the next person and so on down the line.

Good! Let's try this again as we sing the song "Pass it On." When you come to the end of the row the last person reverses the squeeze and it keeps going.

SONG   "Pass It On"

OLD TESTAMENT SCRIPTURE   Psalms 90
Minister: Our first Scripture selection is Psalms 90. We will read responsively. Those on the left side begin with verse 1. The right side will take verse 2 and so on, alternating verses.

NEW TESTAMENT SCRIPTURE   2 Timothy 1:5
Child Reader: Our New Testament Scripture today is from a letter that Paul wrote to his young friend Timothy: "I remember the sincere faith you have, the kind of faith that your grandmother, Lois, and your mother Eunice, also had."

INTERCESSORY PRAYERS
Minister: We, too, are thankful for our grandmothers and the faith they have passed on to us. We want to remember our own grandmothers now in prayer.

Father, we come before you humbly. We pray earnestly now for our grandmothers who have handed down the faith to us. These are special persons we pray for today. (Will you call out the first name of your grandmother so we might bring that loved one into the presence of God?)

[*Minister works spontaneous roll call of names into his prayer.*]

Amen.

HYMN   "Happy the Home When God is There"

SHARING MEMORIES

Minister: We want to take some time now to share memories. Remember when we were reading Psalms 90 together and we read in verse 9, "We spend our years as a tale that is told." Many of our grandparents here today have tales to tell us. Just as Timothy's grandmother, Lois, must have often talked to him, some of our grandmothers are going to share with us what it was like when they were young.

First, we have two readings from a grandmother who remembers these things . . .

Grandma's Safari
by
Louise Neel Gattis

I am a member of that inclusive breed who exclaims most ungrandmaishly, "I am exhausted! My grandchildren have been visiting me. What a joy and what a relief to see them leave."

What is wrong with the grandmothers of this era? They deplete themselves entertaining the grandchildren, rushing them to swimming pools, picture shows, and keeping new tubes in the TV. Still kids are bored and grandma's worn out.

My grandmother didn't expend half the energy we moderns do today, yet I have only to open the memory doors of childhood, and I recall even Grandma's daily tasks took on an aura of excitement. My grandmother could make a simple chore, like going to the henhouse, as exciting as a safari in Africa.

In the Spring, when the maternal instinct reached its peak, she often had as many as ten hens setting. A setting hen can present a terrifying picture with ruffled feathers, sharp beak and unlidded eyes. With Daniel-like bravery she would reach under those squawky, aspiring mothers and remove the fresh unmarked eggs laid by an intruding pullet.

I liked just standing in the doorway holding the wicker egg basket as Grandma went from hen to hen, but when she called Fido and Shep to go with us down the path to the henhouse, both the dogs and I tingled because we knew instinctively something big was about to happen.

This time I stood just outside the door while Grandma stepped calmly over the sill and with the dexterity of a circus performer reached under the silent setting hen and agilely pulled out, by the tail, a six foot chicken snake whose humped body was evidence of an egg thief.

She threw it to the eager barking dogs, who gleefully shook the snake into shreds. Going on to the next nest, she would give the same barehand performance because snakes usually worked in pairs.

The same grandma would return from this event, wash her hands, remove her split bonnet, tie a clean white apron around her waist and say, "Come, Mary Louise, it is time for your catechism lesson."

I don't believe she was ever exhausted by my visit and I know I was never bored.

A Letter About My Grandsons
by
Louise Neel Gattis

Dear Gloria and Judy,

Presenting your father and me with two grandsons makes a brimful, eventful year. Truly "our cup runneth over." My wish is that Paul and Neel may know something of the era in which your father and I grew up. In retrospect we often remember the lovely, but not always.

Hurrah, my grandsons won't be dosed with calomel and be drenched with castor oil. They won't have a flannel cloth soaked in coal oil and lard blister their chests. They won't have to endure long scratchy underwear from October to May or wear long black stockings and high-button shoes. Hurrah, they won't have to lime the privy, read by coal oil lamps, learn the long and short catechism, pick up corn cobs for kindling, eat sulphurated apples, or shoo flies with peacock feathers.

Laments, though, because they will never know the excitement of hog killing time, the magic words of "the thresher is coming," taste delectable cold clabber with crumbled-in cornbread or feel the cleanliness of homemade lye soap. And they probably won't ever know the tastiness of cold fried shoulder meat from an iron skillet between two soft buttermilk biscuits. They won't ever use napkin rings, spoon holders, toothpick holders or chew a slice of homemade bread spread with freshly churned butter. Too, they'll never know the sweetness of blackberry jam spooned from a gallon crock, or feel the breathless excitement of finding a new hen's nest in the barn loft. Laments because they will miss the snugness of slumber with a nightcap on their heads and hot wrapped brick at their feet — in a room around Eskimo temperature. Perhaps when Paul and Neel reach maturity all these things will be considered too simple for enjoyment. And no doubt they'll lament: "If only Grandma and Grandpa could have travelled — at least to the moon."

These laments and hurrahs are the rights of every generation.

SHARING MEMORIES [By grandmothers present]

MEDITATION BY MINISTER [If desired]

OFFERING

CLOSING HYMN   "Faith of Our Fathers"
   [Recession of children with paper chain of faith]

BENEDICTION
   Minister: Father, who abides with each generation, find in our hearts a dwelling place. Go with us as we attempt to be your church in this day. Amen.
                                        — Judy Gattis Smith

ADDITIONAL IDEAS
1. This service prompts a "Celebrating Grandfathers" service, or a service celebrating older persons.
2. How about a "Grandmother — Mother — Daughter Retreat" for a day or a weekend. What a grand way to utilize this service!
3. Plan a time for children to talk about their grandparents and what it is like to be a grandchild — what it is like to have grandparents. Then have the grandparents respond.
4. Plan a time for persons who might not be grandparents of children, but who are grandparents of the community. (Persons who have lived in the community for over 55 years — older persons who are loving and who are loved.)
5. After the service spend time together on a picnic, with outdoor games, making home-made ice cream, or something similar.

David and Goliath

Theme of the Service

One of the unique things about this service is the three-part sermon. The first is the retelling of the story of David and Goliath in a contemporary manner. The second and third sections present the practical application of this biblical message. The result is that the theme of personal strength is woven through the entire service.

One can readily see that this service is planned for families — especially with the children in mind. Not only do they participate in the service through word and song, but the brief meditations are ideal for their interest span. (This is much better than being bored by a long, dry sermon for twenty minutes!)

Directions for the Service

This service was successful and inspirational when it was conducted at Hope Ridge United Methodist Church near Mentor, Ohio. Much of this was due to advance planning and preparation under the direction of Mrs. Marian Reid, Director of Children's Work. The choral reading and Gloria Patri were used in the children's church school classes during the previous month. Thus, they were leaders instead of followers in these sections of the worship service.

The children were seated with their parents for the rythmic reading of Psalms 95. The congregation was divided into two sections, and referred to as Group 1 and Group 2 in the reading. The lines designated *All* were, of course, read by everyone. Prior to the reading, it was important for the leader to call attention to the decrease in the volume of the group.

For the singing of the Gloria Patri, the children gathered in the chancel and lined it for the congregation. Since this version is different from that found in most hymnals, much advance practice was necessary.

Materials/People Needed
1. Group of children (previously trained in choral reading and singing of Gloria Patri.)
2. Choral reading — Psalms 95:1-7. Words in service following. Teaching instructions in Teacher's Guidebook, *Middle Elementary Christian Studies* VCS, 1977, Graded Press, Nashville, Tennessee, p. 28.
3. Gloria Patri (contemporary version) Words and music in Student Book, *Middle Elementary Christian Studies* VCS, 1977, Graded Press, Nashville, Tennessee, p. 23.
4. Special Music — "Bless the Beasts and the Children" by DeVorzon and Botkin
5. Hymns:
    "All People That on Earth Do Dwell — Hymnal
    "Savior, Teach Me, Day by Day" — Hymnal
    "May the Lord Bless and Keep You — (in service)

THE SERVICE

THE GATHERING TIME
[*Parish News, Information, etc.*]

PRELUDE
Lighting of the Candles

CALL TO WORSHIP   Children and Congregation
Rythmic Choral Reading
Psalms 95:1-7
All: O Come, let us sing to the Lord.
[*Louder*]: O Come, let us sing to the Lord.
Group 1: Sing to the Lord, Sing to the Lord, Sing to the Lord.

[*Pause*]

Group 2: Let us make a joyful noise to the rock of our salvation! Let us come into his presence with thanksgiving.

[*Pause*]

All: Let us make a joyful noise to him with songs of praise.

Group 1: For the Lord is a great god,

All: and a great King above all gods.

Group 1: In his hand are the depths of the earth;

Group 2: the heights of the mountains are his also. The sea is his, for he made it.

All: For his hands formed the dry land.

[*Softly*]

Group 1: O come, let us worship and bow down,

Group 2: let us kneel before the Lord, our maker.

All: For he is our God. For he is our God. For he is our God.

Group 2: And we are the people of his pasture,

Group 1: and the sheep of his hand.

Group 2: And we are the people of his pasture,

Group 1: and the sheep of his hand.

All: And we are the people of his pasture,

[*Softer*] and the sheep of his hand.

[*Whisper*] And we are the people of his pasture, and the sheep of his hand.

HYMN   "All People That On Earth Do Dwell"

INVOCATION

CHORAL RESPONSE

SHARING I   "The Story of David and Goliath"

Text   2 Samuel 17:19ff

Most of you know about a man named David, a shepherd boy who worked himself up to being a King of all Israel. Perhaps you know him best as the writer of many songs . . . songs found in a book called Psalms. As a song writer he no doubt was well in the class of a Neal Sidaka or a Neal Diamond and he sang many of his own songs . . . never able to get into the class of Pink Floyd, however. But he did get his lyrics printed in the world's best seller.

There is a story about David as a teenager. It was a time of great armies, kings, battles. It all happened in the Middle East where you now read of many battles and military events.

Well, it seems that Israel — that was the nation of which David was a citizen — was at war with a nation called the Philistines. David had several brothers who were a part of the army and like armies of that day their food supply was furnished by their families quite often. So Jesse, the father, sent his son, David, to his brothers with food.

Shortly after David arrived at the place where the army was in camp, there seemed to be some kind of disturbance out near the front lines. When David arrived, he saw a huge man. The giant shouted his own name — "Goliath" — and he dared someone to come out and fight him. This giant was pretty awesome and no one seemed to want to do it . . . not even a company of soldiers seemed to want to take him on.

David was a pretty loyal patriot of Israel, and he could not understand why this man — even if he were a huge giant — could frighten his nation's army. Was not God with Israel?

So, as the story goes, he spoke up that he would fight Goliath. Well, Saul who was king of Israel, heard it and called him to his tent. David's brothers had urged him to be quiet, to keep still lest he get in trouble. This did not stop him; he entered Saul's tent and repeated his words.

Saul looked at this young fellow and said, "You are inexperienced in fighting: you have no weapons; you have no armor." "I still want to go," said David. Saul finally consented and suggested that David put on his heavy metal armor.

Well, David tried it, but it was so heavy he could hardly move and his knees felt as if they would buckle. It was kind of funny to see this young man stumble and stagger about in the king's tent.

So off came the armor and David started out toward the giant dressed only in an animal loin cloth with a sling shot hung on the side. He did stop at a stream and selected five smooth stones before he continued his march towards Goliath.

Goliath growled in his deep voice, taunting the Israelites that they would send a boy against him . . . He promised to destroy the lad and then march on the Israelites.

But David continued to approach him . . . Then as they drew near, David selected one of his smooth stones, placed it in his sling shot, whirled the small leather pouch over his head and then let loose of one side of the pouch . . . and the stone whirled, tore through the air in the direction of Goliath. Goliath by this time had raised his sword and was rumbling down towards the lad called David.

Well, that stone flew straight and strong . . . and that stone hit the forehead of the Giant . . . one more faltering step and he fell heavily to the ground . . . The giant Goliath had been defeated and David, the young lad, had become victor.

PASTORAL PRAYER

HYMN   "Savior, Teach Me, Day by Day"

SHARING II   "Goliath Is What Kind of Enemy?"

The story of David and Goliath, of course, was told at the camp fires of Israelites to inspire bravery and courage, much as our hero stories are told.

I couldn't help asking the question, "What does Goliath stand for . . . Who was the enemy?"

It is mighty easy in our day to develop a lot of enemies . . . real ones and imaginary ones. Would you believe, when I was small and my parents would not allow me to do something I wanted to do, I thought they were my enemy?

How often, when we disagree with someone, it doesn't just stop with disagreement . . . we think of that person as our enemy.

How difficult it is to see people . . . people with different styles of living, wearing different clothes, having a different language . . . it is easy not to see them as people, but it is easy to see them as THE ENEMY.

Who are your enemies? That's not a bad question to ask. Not so that you can add to the list of your enemies . . . it is a good question because we may be mistaking something very normal and a part of life as an enemy. We may be drawing up sides rather than working together for something meaningful.

Who is your enemy? This is a question that our world needs to ask itself quite often. The riots in Watts and the hangings of the old West are examples of how often society turns upon the wrong person. David's question in this story is a good one — WHO IS THIS PERSON?

Not always is our enemy a person . . . IT'S JUST A GIANT . . . A HUGE FORCE AT WORK. But we really won't know unless we ask the question WHO IS MY ENEMY?

VOCAL SELECTION   "Bless the Beasts and the Children"

SHARING III   "David Is What Kind of Power?"

I titled this third part of the story, "DAVID IS WHAT KIND OF POWER?" It would probably be better to have said: "Where does my power come from when I face an enemy?"

1. It is pretty obvious that David recognized right off that he was not powerless. Too many of us have run out on life. Faith is poking holes in a solid wall and gleefully saying, "By golly, there is more than one view of the other side."

Those brothers of David and the other soldiers saw Goliath and said: "We can't do anything about it . . ." Faith is not just an emotional feeling — it is an inner confidence that there are choices, things can change. It is easy to lose your faith in this kind of world. Goliaths come in many forms . . . a tough assignment in class . . . a routine monotonous job, an illness, a failure, a great loss . . . a shift of gear. If several Goliaths hit you at once, the most normal reaction is to just throw up your hands. I know, I have done it.

I like the man in the New Testament who said to Jesus as he faced his Goliath — a physical problem — "I believe, help my unbelief." Don't let my discouragement . . . don't let my fear . . . don't let my anxiety rule me . . . I will accept that it is there and real but don't let it rule me.

2. Then David does something that I think we all need to do. I forget the singer but his song sticks in my mind — "I'll do it my way." David would have been a farce if he had tried to go out and fight Goliath in Saul's armor . . . even with God helping him.

I believe that the energy of faith is more often hampered because we try to put it into some style, or form, or dress of somebody else. That's putting on Saul's armor and it's just dead wrong to try it and the words dead wrong is to say exactly what it means . . .

It would probably have been even sillier if he had sought to go out and wrestle with Goliath. He evaluated his skills, he sensed the weapons he had and he faced the situation as David.

Our strength lies in knowing we are not powerless. Our strength lies in knowing clearly the alternatives that exist and our strength lies in being ourselves in attacking the Giant . . . using our natural skills . . . our God given qualities.

QUIET TIME [*Organ meditations*]

SERVICE OF STEWARDSHIP
Offertory
Gloria Patri [*Lined by the children*]
"Praise the God who made us,
And Jesus Christ,
And praise the Spirit, too.
Love was here in the beginning.
It is now and ever shall be
Love without end. Amen. Amen."

PRAYER

BENEDICTION HYMN   (Tune — Edelweiss)
"May the Lord, mighty God,
Bless and keep you forever;
Grant you peace, perfect peace,
Courage in every endeavor.
Lift up your eyes and see his face,
And his grace forever.
May the Lord, mighty God,
Bless and keep you forever. Amen."
                                    — R. M. Lautenschlager
POSTLUDE

ADDITIONAL IDEAS
1. Use puppets to tell the story of David and Goliath.
2. Have children of a church school class act out the story in the chancel.
3. Use David and Goliath to open discussion of feelings and behavior. What is a "swagger?" When you

swagger, how do you feel? Have you ever heard anyone "growl?" How did it make you feel?

4. Relate masks to the concept of "strangers" and "the enemy." Remove the masks and become friends.

5. Develop the idea of fear and the unknown. When we are surrounded by darkness, or even shadows, we often become afraid. When the light is turned on — or we receive more information about the thing we fear — we are no longer afraid.

6. Create a "Giant" in preparation for this service. It might be in the form of one of the following:
   a. A large papier-mache giant.
   b. An enormous, piercing sound.
   c. Many slides of "giant structures" projected on the walls of sanctuary, or on multi-surface screens such as large, white mobiles.

7. Plan a retreat, for children or families, using David and Goliath as the theme and developing the ideas in the story.

A Celebration of Life

Theme of the Service

Let's celebrate life — not just our own, but all life around us. Following this theme, the service is designed to have our own life take on new meaning for us. We hope that many worshipers will develop a new sense of appreciation for the highest form of life — that which comes to us as we permit the spirit of Christ to enter into our lives.

While it may seem strange to bring animals and birds into the sanctuary, they are important to our realization of the greatness of life that God has created. They also help to make this service one which the children will remember for a long time to come. The first chapter of Genesis will not seem far off and unrelated to those who share in this worship experience.

Directions for the Service

To be most effective, this service should be held in the evening. This is necessary to effectively portray the "giving of light" into the world with a spotlight. This will also highlight the "gifts of life" as they are brought to the chancel.

This service will take a great deal of advance preparation. The children who bring the "gifts of life" to the chancel will need to be selected carefully. Some items will require tall children or youth. Those who bring pets should be cautioned about the care of them before and after the service. (Imagine the excitement of trying to catch a hampster which has escaped from his cage, or trying to trap a parakeet flying through the sanctuary!)

A long narrow table should be placed in a prominent location in the chancel, to be used for the placing of the "gifts of life." It could be directly in front of the altar but somewhat lower so the children will have no difficulty in placing the items on it. A wire should be strung across the chancel above the table. This will provide a place to hang the earth, sun, and moon in the service.

Three items will need to be made beforehand. These are the sun, moon, and earth, which can be easily made of paper mache placed over balloons. A church school class or junior high youth group would enjoy making these.

Three choirs are suggested to sing the hymns in "The Praise and Celebration of Life." Instead of using a children's choir, the children's hymns might be presented by one or more church school classes. The music may be adapted to that available in your particular church, with familiar hymns substituted for unknown ones. However, the ones used were chosen for the correlation of the words of specific stanzas to the words of Scripture.

The Scripture passages may be read by eight young people or by one narrator. If you want to use a large number of participants, here is a good place to use high school youth who do not sing in the choir. Of course, all of the passages could be read by the pastor.

The "Giving of Our Gifts" segment near the end of the service is designed to give the congregation an opportunity to express appreciation of the gifts of life. They may desire to respond with an offering; some persons may want to make a gift of time or self, and slips of paper should be provided on which these items can be written. Of course, they may be placed in the offering plate as it is passed.

Materials/People Needed
  1. Pastor
  2. Eight narrators (Scripture)
  3. Children's choral group
  4. Youth choir

5. Adult choir
6. Eleven children (Gifts of life)
7. Mother and small baby
8. Long narrow table
9. Wire strung above table
10. Bible (Revised Standard Version)
11. Earth
12. Spotlight
13. Two glass pitchers of water
14. Flowering plant
15. Bowl of fruit
16. Sun
17. Moon
18. Tropical fish (in bowl)
19. Parakeet or canary
20. Gerbil or hampster
21. Picture of Jesus
22. Choral reading (Psalms 104)
23. Hymns:
"Praise to the Lord, the Almighty"
"God of the Earth, the Sky, the Sea"
"The Heavens Declare Thy Glory, Lord"
"This Is My Father's World"
"All Creatures of Our God and King"
"All Things Bright and Beautiful"
"For the Beauty of the Earth"
"I Heard the Voice of Jesus Say"

THE SERVICE

THE PRELUDE

THE CALL TO WORSHIP
Pastor: The earth is the Lord's and the fullness
thereof; the world and they that dwell therein.

People: O Lord, our Lord, how excellent is your name in all the earth.

Pastor: O come, let us worship and bow down; let us kneel before the Lord our maker.

People: Let us praise him for his mighty deeds; let us praise him according to his exceeding greatness.

THE HYMN OF PRAISE "Praise to the Lord, the Almighty"

THE COLLECT [*In unison*]

Lord of all creation, who has given life to all things on this earth and beyond: Grant that we may not only celebrate your gift of life through our words of praise, but that we may also develop a new appreciation of all things which you have created and resolve to preserve and protect all forms of life; in the name of Jesus Christ we pray. Amen.

Praise and Celebration of Life

IN THE BEGINNING

Genesis 1:1-5

[*1st reader*]

In the beginning God created the heavens and the earth. [*Tall child or youth places earth on wire near altar.*] The earth was without form and void, and darkness was upon the face of the deep; and the Spirit of God was moving over the face of the waters. And God said, "Let there be light;" [*Turn spotlight on earth and area where objects will be placed*] and there was light. And God saw that the light was good; and God separated the light from the darkness. God called the light Day, and the darkness he called Night. And there was evening and there was morning, one day.

The Hymn [*Adult choir*] "God of the Earth, the Sky, the Sea"

SEPARATION OF THE WATERS
The Scripture Genesis 1:6-8
[*2nd reader*]

And God said, "Let there be a firmanment in the midst of the waters, and let it separate the waters from the waters." [*Two children approach table with each carrying glass pitcher of water. Each places his pitcher at extreme end of the table*]. And God made the firmament and separated the waters which were under the firmament from the waters which were above the firmament. And it was so. And God called the firmament Heaven. And there was evening and there was morning, a second day.

The Hymn "The Heavens Declare Thy Glory, Lord" [*Youth choir*]

FORMATION OF PLANTS AND TREES
The Scripture Genesis 1:9-13
[*3rd reader*]

And God said, "Let the waters under the heavens be gathered together into one place, and let the dry land appear. And it was so. God called the dry land Earth, and the waters that were gathered together he called Seas. And God saw that it was good. And God said, "Let the earth put forth vegetation, (and) plants yielding seed.

[*Child carries flowering plant and places it on table.*]

And God said, "Let the earth put forth . . . fruit trees bearing fruit in which is their seed, each according to its kind, upon the earth." And it was so.

[*Child carries bowl of fruit and places it on table.*]

The earth brought forth vegetation, plants yielding seed according to their own kinds, and trees bearing fruit in which is their seed, each according to its kind. And God saw that it was good. And there was evening and there was morning, a third day.

The Hymn   "This is My Father's World"
[Congregation]

THE SUN AND MOON APPEAR
The Scripture   Genesis 1:14-19
[4th reader]

And God said, "Let there be lights in the firmament of the heavens to separate the day from the night; and let them be for signs and for seasons and for days and years, and let them be lights in the firmament of the heavens to give light upon the earth." And it was so. And God made two great lights, the greater light to rule the day, and the lesser light to rule the night; he made the stars also.

[*One tall child, or youth, places sun on wire to the left of earth, while second child places moon to the right.*]

And God set them in the firmament of the heavens to give light upon the earth, to rule over the day and over the night, and to separate the light from the darkness. And God saw that it was good. And there was evening and there was morning, a fourth day.

The Hymn   "All Creatures of Our God and King"
[Children's choir]

CREATURES OF THE SEA AND AIR COME FORTH
The Scripture   Genesis 1:20-23
[5th reader]

And God said, "Let the waters bring forth swarms of living creatures, and let birds fly above the earth across the firmament of the heavens." So God created the great sea monsters, and every living creature that moves, with which the waters swarm, according to their kinds.

[*Child places fish bowl, containing several tropical fish, on table.*]

So God created . . . every winged bird according to its kind. And God saw that it was good.

[*Child places small cage, containing parakeet or canary on table.*]

And God blessed them, saying, "Be fruitful and multiply and fill the waters in the seas, and let birds multiply on the earth." And there was evening and there was morning, a fifth day.

The Hymn   "All Things Bright and Beautiful"
                    [*Children's choir*]

LIVING CREATURES INHABIT THE EARTH
The Scripture   Genesis 1:24-25
                    [*6th reader*]

And God said, "Let the earth bring forth living creatures according to their kinds: cattle and creeping things and beasts of the earth according to their kinds." And it was so. And God made the beasts of the earth according to their kinds and the cattle according to their kinds, and everything that creeps upon the earth according to its kind. And God saw that it was good.

[*Child takes cage, containing gerbil or hampster, and places it on table.*]

The Choral Reading   Psalm 104:1, 10-20, 24, 35
                    [*Youth choir*]

All: Bless the Lord, O my soul!
     O Lord my God, thou art very great!
Girls: Thou makest springs gush forth in the valleys;
     They flow between the hills.
Boys: They give drink to every beast of the field;
     The wild asses quench their thirst.
Girls: By them the birds of the air have their habitation;
     They sing among the branches.
All: From thy lofty abode thou waterest the mountains;
     The earth is satisfied with the fruit of thy work.

Boys: Thou dost cause the grass to grow for the cattle,
And plants for man to cultivate.
Girls: That he may bring forth food from the earth,
And wine to gladden the heart of man,
Oil to make his face shine,
And bread to strengthen man's heart.
Boys: The trees of the Lord are watered abundantly,
The cedars of Lebanon which he planted.
Girls: In them the birds build their nests;
The stork has her home in the fir trees.
Boys: The high mountains are for the wild goats;
The rocks are a refuge for the badgers.
Girls: Thou hast made the moon to mark the seasons;
The sun knows its time for setting.
Boys: Thou makest darkness, and it is night,
When all the beasts of the forest creep forth.
All: O lord, how manifold are thy works!
In wisdom hast thou made them all;
The earth is full of thy creatures.
Bless the Lord, O my soul!
Praise the Lord!

THE CREATION OF MANKIND
The Scripture   Genesis 1:26-31
[*7th reader*]

Then God said, "Let us make man in our image, after our likeness; and let them have dominion over the fish of the sea, and over the birds of the air, and over the cattle, and over all the earth, and over every creeping thing that creeps upon the earth." So God created man in his own image, in the image of God he created him; male and female he created them.

[*Mother carries small baby forward and is seated in chair near table containing other living things.*]

And God blessed them, and God said to them, "Be fruitful and multiply, and fill the earth and subdue it;

and have dominion over the fish of the sea and over the birds of the air and over every living thing that moves upon the earth." And God said, "Behold, I have given you every plant yielding seed which is upon the -face of all the earth, and every tree with seed in its fruit; you shall have them for food. And to every beast of the earth, and to every bird of the air, and to everything that creeps on the earth, everything that has the breath of life, I have given every green plant for food." And it was so. And God saw everything that he had made, and behold, it was very good. And there was evening and there was morning, a sixth day.

The Hymn   "For the Beauty of the Earth"
                    [Congregation]

THE GIFT OF ABUNDANT LIFE
The Scripture   John 1:1-5, 9-12
                    [8th reader]
In the beginning was the Word, and the Word was with God, and the Word was God. He was in the beginning with God; all things were made through him, and without him was not anything made that was made. In him was life, and the life was the light of men. The light shines in the darkness, and the darkness has not overcome it.

The true light that enlightens every man was coming into the world. He was in the world, and the world was made through him, yet the world knew him not. He came to his own home, and his own people received him not. But to all who received him, who believed in his name, he gave power to become children of God.

[Child places picture of Jesus at very center of table, or on the altar.]

The Narration
                    [8th reader]
Jesus said, "I came that (you) might have life, and

have it abundantly." He came into the world, not for his own sake, but for all mankind. When we become discouraged and burdened with the problems of life we hear him say, "Come to me, all who labor and are heavy laden, and I will give you rest." We can face the future unafraid when we realize that we will be directed to new life ahead by the one who said, "I am the light of the world." While we receive many hours of joy and happiness in life upon this earth, he came to tell us of an even greater life beyond. As we permit his Spirit to enter into our lives, he says that this will become in us "a spring of water welling up to eternal life."

The Hymn   "I Heard the Voice of Jesus Say"
                         [*Adult choir*]

THE GIVING OF OUR GIFTS
        Pastor: as an expression of our appreciation to Almighty God for his marvelous gifts of life, we will now present our gifts to him.
[*Gifts of substance, time or self, written on slips of paper, may be placed in offering plate.*]

THE OFFERTORY

THE DOXOLOGY

THE PRAYER OF DEDICATION

THE HYMN OF DEDICATION   "God, Who Touchest Earth
                              With Beauty"

THE BENEDICTION

THE POSTLUDE

                         — Ralph E. Dessem

ADDITIONAL IDEAS
1. The lighting for this service is critical. Why not design your own dimmer panel and utilize various spots to focus on the items of special interest? The service might be concluded with a spot on the cross and the picture of Jesus.
2. Interpretive dance could be used effectively during the singing of one or two hymns, such as "All Creatures of our God and King" and "All Things Bright and Beautiful."
3. The use of different readers, rather than just one or two, makes it possible to have readers in various locations in the sanctuary. This will provide added variety and interest.
4. Costumes could be used for the children if they were imaginative and well constructed. For instance, a child could wear a large mask of the sun and be robed in gold. The moon costume could include a white or yellow mask with a dark blue robe. Children could wear masks representing the heads of animals and be dressed in costumes of the appropriate colors. If the costumes are well done, this might stimulate groups to consider other dramatic vehicles which could utilize the costumes (i.e. Benjamin Britten's, The Ark).
5. In "The Giving of Our Gifts," persons could be encouraged to write their "gifts to God" on slips of paper and place in sealed envelopes. Each might identify his envelope with a symbol, or name, and place it on the altar. The envelopes could remain there for some time — six to twelve months. However, at any time, a person could take his envelope, open it, and add gifts to his list. The envelopes could also be returned to the "givers" at a specific time (if names were on them) to remind them of their intentions.

The Weight of the Stones

Theme of the Service

One aspect of church life gaining in popularity is the family camp or weekend retreat for families. The leisure of this type of situation provides a unique opportunity for people to interact in a meaningful, loving way. This is especially true with parent-child relationships. Away from the hurry and stress of daily routine, families can develop the sort of caring community which becomes a highlight of the year.

This service, which was used with a Disciples of Christ group in Michigan, is designed to close a week of family camp or weekend retreat. It is intended to celebrate the joy of the week, or weekend, and to address the issue of how families can take the experience home. It will be most effective if conducted in an outdoor setting.

Directions for the Service

For this service to be effective, there are several important things necessary in the planning and preparation:

1. Assign a family or a committee composed of people of all ages to prepare and lead the worship service. This family/committee has responsibility for selecting an appropriate setting for worship as well as deciding ways to highlight the events, feelings, program of study, and the like, which were peculiar to the group's week. As this service must be adapted to the situation and experience of the group, it is written with many suggestions. The family/committee has full responsibility for "personalizing" it.

2. This service requires a large collection of stones. They should be about the size of a fist. If they are not available, books or some other items of equal size and weight may be substituted. If stones are scarce at the

campground, the family/committee should provide a large number of stones, or substitutes, on the table in the front of the worship area.

3. The following announcement (in effect) should be made to the entire group several hours in advance of the service:

"For our closing worship tonight each family (or each person if the group is small enough) is asked to bring one item which they feel represents what was 'special' about his week. For instance, you might bring a cup of water from the lake, a flower from the woods, a plate from the dining hall, or a hymnal from the chapel. You may decide that what was best about this week was the opportunity to laugh together, to be forgiven, or to forgive someone else. Use your collective imagination. Bring something to worship tonight which you feel represents the very best of the week."

Before the service begins, each family will be asked to bring its particular item and place it on the altar or table. The result may be a variety of things such as: sporting equipment (for the fun we had together), wrist watches (for the time we had for one another), Bibles (for the opportunity of worship and study), etc.

Materials Needed
1. Large stones, or substitutes, for each person.
2. Altar, or table (for items of significance)
3. The Living Bible
4. Hymns and Songs:
    "For the Beauty of the Earth"
    "God, Who Touchest Earth With Beauty"
    "This is My Father's World"
    "Take My Life and Let It Be Consecrated"
    "Ain't Goin' to Study War No More"
    "Bridge Over Troubled Waters"
    "He's Got the Whole World in His Hands"
    "I'd Like to Teach the World to Sing"

"Love is the Answer"
"Tell Me Why"
"They'll Know We Are Christians by Our Love"

THE SERVICE

PREPARATION

[*The leader should ask each person, or family representative, to explain the significance of what they brought to the worship service. When they have explained how it represents the best of the week, the item should be placed on the altar, or table, at the front of the worship area.*]

CALL TO WORSHIP

[*A leader in front and other members of family/committee dispersed through the congregation. Each stands to read his/her part.*]
Leader: This is a place the Lord has made!
Voice 1: It is a place of beauty.
Voice 2: A place of trees and flowers.
Voice 3: Of hills and valleys.
Leader: This is a week the Lord has given us!
Voice 1: It has been a week of singing and laughing.
Voice 2: A week of playing and talking.
Voice 3: Of study and prayer.
Leader: We know that the Lord is in this place!
Voice 1: We have felt his presence in our fellowship.
Voice 2: In our times of study and times of play.
Voice 3: For as we come to care for one another, we come to know God. For God is love!

INVOCATION

"Father, it has been good this week. We have taken time with one another. In the hurry of routine we don't always do that. We have listened more intently to the joys and hurts of one another. In the rush of school and work we don't always listen so carefully. We have forgiven more quickly and laughed more easily at our faults. At home it is not easy to forgive and laugh at ourselves. We take too seriously our roles of strong parents and rebellious children. It has been a good week for we have taken the time to care a little more, to give a little extra, to love more deeply. Father, don't let us stop now! Amen."

SONG FEST
[The theme of the singing should emphasize the the positive. Here are some suggestions.]
"I'd Like to Teach the World To Sing"
"This Is My Father's World"
"For The Beauty of The Earth"
"Tell Me Why"

PREPARATION FOR EVENING PRAYER
[Asking questions is a very simple way of directing thoughts toward prayer. This is especially effective with children. The leader may conduct a running dialogue with the children by asking them what made them laugh, smile, or cry during the week. What happened that made them feel forgiven, happy or sad? Where is their favorite place in camp? Their favorite event? For what are they most thankful?]

EVENING PRAYER
[The comments made by the children should be incorporated into the evening prayer. These will be ordinary things. The point is that we come to know one another better; love one another more; experience the Transcendent more significantly in the ordinary events of life. The prayer should

emphasize our need to listen more carefully, watch more closely, and tune our sensors more toward feeling what is happening in the lives of those closest to us. To overlook the ordinary is to overlook some of the most important events of Life.]

HOMILY

[*Some suggestions for a short meditation include*]:

"The Caring Community" Acts 2:44-47

This has been a week in which we have been like the early church. We have shared everything. Give thanks for the opportunity.

"The Gentle Sound of Stillness" 1 Kings 19:1-12

Elijah discovered that God spoke more clearly after the wind, the earthquake, and the fire. God spoke in the gentle sound of silence. For those who attune their hearts and minds, God speaks most clearly in the gentle stillness of ordinary events.

"Happy Because We Are His" Psalms 100 (Living Bible)

What makes for happiness? It is not what we have done or what we acquire. Happiness comes because of whose we are!

SONG FEST

"Love Is The Answer"
"They'll Know We are Christians By Our Love"
"God, Who Touchest Earth With Beauty"
"He's Got the Whole World In His Hands"

LAYING DOWN THE STONES

[*The intent of this worship activity is to demonstrate how some problems develop in daily home life, i.e., we collect too many "stones" which we insist on carrying with us. Ask the congregation to disperse and find a stone about the size of a fist. If this is not pracitcal, ask them to come to the*

table/altar where a large supply has been gathered.]
Leader: I want each of you to hold your stone at arm's length. Consider if you can answer "yes" to any of these questions.
[*Leader speaks slowly so the stones will grow heavier.*]
Do you ever say, "Well, I will forgive, but I can never forget!"?
Are you ever secretly happy when something unfortunate happens to others?
When someone in the family hurts you, do you try to get even?
Do you sulk and refuse to talk when hurt or angry?
When you have an argument with your brother/sister/husband/wife/parents/children do you bring up things done in the past?
Is there someone in the family you resent because he/she is better looking, smarter, more popular, or whatever?
Do you spend too much of your time worrying about what might happen?
By now the stone you are carrying is getting heavy. Lay it down. Doesn't that feel better? Usually we don't carry real stones around with us. That is foolish. Stones are useless weights.
Yet we willingly carry other kinds of "stones." We carry around anger, resentment, and plans for revenge. We take out our frustrations on those closest to us. We worry ourselves into paralysis. We sulk and give one another the "silent treatment." Then we wonder why our home life is not as good as it could be.
We are too willing to carry the "stones" of anger, resentment, frustration and worry. They are as useless and foolish to keep as the stones you have been holding.

SONG FEST
>"Ain't Goin' To Study War No More"
>"Take My Life and Let It Be Consecrated"
>"Bridge Over Troubled Waters"

THE DISMISSAL
>O God who brought us together this week in love and molded us into a caring community, we give you thanks. Hear our prayer that the "stones" we gather may not be carried long. Grant us your grace that we might seek and grant forgiveness more easily. May we direct our anger and frustrations in ways which will not hurt others. May we feel no need to sulk or seek revenge. Heavenly Father, we know that if we find ways to relieve ourselves of the unnecessary burden of these useless "stones," our life together will be more blessed.
>
>>Now, may the peace of God go with us.
>>May the love we shared this week
>>Become commonplace in our homes, our work, our play.
>>May great joy permeate all we do and say."
>>>Amen and Amen.

>>>— R. Robert Cueni

ADDITIONAL IDEAS
1. Arrange to have different families or individuals discuss the weight of the "stones" they accumulate in their family. This may be done while the rest of the congregation is holding their stones outstretched. Have persons discuss particular incidents, or confess to family ways of handling situations which permit the weight of "stones" to accumulate. They should conclude by describing effective ways of laying down their "stones," i.e., effective ways of handling anger, frustration, sulking, etc.

2. Assign a family, or group, the task of using this idea of "stones" to discuss a typical family problem. For instance, have a family role-play a scene on *worry*. As older members of the family act out the scene, the youngest child gives stones to the other members. By the end of the scene, everyone is carrying a full lead of stones. Worry is carrying around a useless load of "stones." We learn to lay down the useless burden when we practice the demand of faith to ". . . not worry about tomorrow; it will have enough worries of its own." (Matthew 6:34 TEV)

3. A family role-play has many possibilities. For instance, anger is an additive emotion. Little irritations accumulate until someone in the family explodes. To lay down the "stone of anger" people need to learn how to "be angry, but sin not." (Ephesians 4:26 KJV) (or) Guilt is a heavy load of "stones." Forgiveness by God and those we have offended is the only way to get rid of the load. (or) Refusing to forgive those who have offended you is asking for the chance to carry a load of useless "stones."

Pass It On

Theme of the Service

This service is built around the theme of spreading the word. All of the persons present, children as well as adults, are invited to be proclaimers or newscasters of the word. All are invited to share in this role in a unique way. One member of each family is invited to write a personal message of "good news" on a small card which is attached to a helium filled balloon. Thus, the "word" is spread to many unknown readers.

The three-part sermon (with three songs interspersed) stresses that sometimes it only takes a word from us about God and or faith, like a spark, to get the fire of faith and hope going in someone else's heart. An underlying emphasis of the service is that the church is really a joyful place to be. We need to laugh more in the church, and be reverently childish at times.

Directions for the Service

The tenor of this service was festive when it was originally conducted at St. Peter's United Church of Christ in Elmhurst, Illinois. It was well planned, and the anticipation mounted as the service pogressed. The result was that the adults, as well as the children and youth, were excited about it and this excitement lingered long afterward.

While, in this case, the sermon was interspersed with three songs sung by the minister, who provided his own guitar accompaniment, it could be adapted to a variety of local situations.

At the conclusion of the sermon, ushers distributed helium-filled balloons and cards to family units. The minister encouraged one member of each family to write a personal note on one side of the card. It might be about how important God was to them, or how they were feeling by being in church, etc. Persons who had difficulty composing a message were encouraged to write their address and phone number.

The cards had the following message mimeographed on the other side:

On this Sunday, ...(date)..... , during our joyful family worship service, we sent scores of messages like this aloft. We hope it finds you well and happy, and we want to let you know that coming to church this morning to worship God is what makes us happy. On the other side is a personal message from some family here at
(St. Peter's United Church of Christ
121 W. Church St.
Elmhurst, Illinois 60126)

A long string was attached to each of the helium-filled balloons before they were distributed. Each family was asked to take the other end of the string and tie it to their card (through hole already provided in top of card.) Several of the balloons escaped to the ceiling of the sanctuary in this process, which gave the custodian a real challenge!

During the singing of the final stanza of the last hymn, the congregation moved to the parking lot for the "balloon ascent." Following the words of departure the balloons were released in a group and provided a beautiful sight — a fitting climax to a service that will long be remembered by all who participated.

(One reply to this service came from a man who lived sixty miles away in Indiana. He found the balloon and note in his cornfield, and wrote back how delighted he was to find it.)

Materials needed
1. Balloons (one for each family)

2. Helium (more than enough for balloons)
3. Long pieces of string
4. Message cards (mimeographed note)
5. Guitar (or other instrument to accompany songs)
6. Songs:

> "Lord, I Love to Stomp and Shout"
> — *Songs of Life and Faith*, Pilgrim Press
> "Each Winter as the Year Grows Older"
> — *Hymnal of the United Church of Christ*
> "Pass It On"
> — *Hymns For Now III*, Concordia Publishing House

THE SERVICE

PRELUDE

HYMN   "Lord, Speak to Me That I May Speak"

RESPONSIVE PROCLAMATION
> *Minister:* The Lord is King and rules all people.
> *People:* Both proud and humble together shall worship him.
> *Minister:* Our children, too, shall serve him.
> *People:* For they shall hear from us about the wonders of the Lord.

GLORIA PATRI

COMMUNITY PRAYER [*in unison*]
> God, we do say "thank you" for being so good to us. We would like to let others know about this. In coming here, in singing, and in the other events of this worship service, we hope to be newscasters spreading the word about how important you are to us. Amen

GREETING

Minister: I welcome you this morning with a hearty "Good morning."

People: Good Morning.

Minister: Our theme this morning is spreading the word. I thought of using the title, "Gospeling, Not Gossiping." Gossiping can be spreading a bad word, but gospeling is spreading the good word, or as we say, the good news, which is what gospel means. The good word, or good news, for Christians is that God loves us so much that he sent Jesus, his Son, to live on earth for us, so that we might come to love God even more, so we could know that when we love God nothing can keep us from him — not even death. It is a happy duty of those of us who feel God's presence in our life to let others know about it. Jesus himself taught us to do this. We are to be proclaimers or newscasters. That's not always an easy job. Sometimes we wonder if anyone will, or does, listen to us. Jesus had something to say about being a newscaster of his gospel.

SCRIPTURE   Luke 8:4-15 (paraphrase)

PRAYER

OFFERING

MESSAGE [*in sermon and song*]

When I was saying evening prayers with my little four year old girl this summer she asked me, "Daddy, who is God's mother? Who is mother God?" I tried to explain that God didn't have a wife, which is what she was asking. She became tearful. "No, Daddy, God has to have a wife," she pleaded. Well, it's hard to explain God so a child will understand, isn't it? I heard of one girl recently who wondered if mother nature was God's wife! There are lots of things about God which we don't understand very well, and which puzzle.

But, there are some things we know for sure. One of them is that God loves us very much. For example, did you know, kids, that God is really interested in everything you do? He is. It may seem like a big job, but God knows everybody's name, including yours, and he is interested in you. He sees you grow up strong, and it makes him happy. He knows how you like to play and have fun and that makes him cheerful. He is aware of you learning new things, how you are becoming smarter and wiser, and that delights him. God is also interested in something else about you. Listen to this song where a young person is talking to God.

Song: "Lord, I Love to Stomp and Shout"

Yes, God, too, is interested in what you will become. He knows you will be many things: a husband or wife, a mother or father, a friend to others, a businessman, teacher, doctor, minister. He also hopes that you will be someone who loves him. If you ask someone you don't know, "Who are you?" he usually answers by telling you his name, where he lives, and maybe what he does. Wouldn't you be surprised if you asked, "Who are you?", and the person said, "Well, first I'm a Christian." Whatever it is you're cut out to be, God wants you to feel so much a part of him that you will call yourself a Christian, one who follows him. You don't have to wait until you're grown up to be what Jesus wants you to be. And you don't have to wait until you're grown up to let other people know you think about God, that you go to church, and that you like to be here. When you do that, you, too, are a newscaster, spreading the good news and that makes God happy.

Unfortunately none of us stays as innocent and full of zest as children. We all grow older. This guitar has grown older. At one time it, too, was bouncy and strong, and I looked forward to many years of its sounding alive and happy. But lately it's been nearly impossible to keep it in tune. No matter how much you fiddle with it, what used to be a beautiful sound now seems sour and out of joint. It is as if the guitar is getting tired, that it has worked too long and hard, and that it has lost some of its spirit and vibrancy.

That happens to some people, too. They start out young and hopeful, with a song in their hearts, but as they get older, rather than becoming mellow, their song and hopes become lifeless, even sour. Our muscles might not be as responsive as they used to be; our dreams might be filled with frustrated wishes and sad memories; nothing may excite us any more; we may feel very bad that we did not become what we thought we were cut out to be; and what we once knew to be important and valuable may have become shaken and untrue for us. This happens to everybody at sometime and to some degree. It's part of being human, I suppose. But being human is more than running out of physical or spiritual juice; God has not left us desolate and without inner strength.

Song: "Each Winter As the Year Grows Older"

That is God's gift to us, that no matter how low we get, buried deep within us is the eternal flame of hope. We cannot help hoping and expecting that things will get better. God has so created us that we are resilient; we bounce back. We can catch our breath and be newly re-created by faith. It takes work, just as it took work on my guitar to restore it. It means keeping your spiritual life in good shape, exercising your faith so it will remain strong. Probably nothing helps more than articulating your faith to someone else. Not only does the good news spread when you make it known, but it spreads inside you as well. Blessed are both the listener and the giver.

A word, you know, has a lot of power. When you speak it, it has the potential to transform you as well as the one you speak it to. Sometimes the word — a short careless word — can leave a scar on someone's heart for life. That old saying, "Sticks and stones may break my bones, but words can never hurt me," is untrue. The real saying should be, "Sticks and stones can break my bones but words can break my heart." Words are powerful enough to hurt. But they can heal as well. Jesus himself is called "The Word." He is the one who brings healing to us, as a refreshing word does.

Don't ever think that the word you speak to someone about God and your faith is worthless or ineffective. So very much of God's work is done through simple, down-to-earth words. God works more through the ordinary than through the extraordinary. Each word which you might share with another about your feeling for God and his church is a spark which could kindle a fire in someone's life. Never underestimate it.

Song: "Pass It On"

And you are going to have a chance to pass it on, and in a way you probably haven't done before. Spreading God's word, while important, can also be great fun. I'm convinced that God likes to laugh and have a good time, and that he would be pleased if proclaiming his goodness could be a happy affair. In our Scripture today, Jesus tells us we never know where the word is going to land; and neither will the word you are going to send this morning.

DISTRIBUTION OF BALLOONS [See directions]

HYMN   "Fling Out The Banner"

RECESSIONAL TO PARKING LOT

SERVICE OF ASCENT
  Words of Departure [*Minister*]
      And now let us all, as children of God, send his
      word and spirit abroad.
  RELEASE OF BALLOONS

— Robert L. Randall

ADDITIONAL IDEAS
1. Conduct the service at sunset as a vesper service, using a campfire. Time the service so the balloons are released at dusk. Remain around the fire singing and telling stories. At close of evening, lift up the theme, "It only takes a spark . . . "
2. Take the service and use it as a basis for a retreat for youth, adults, or youth and adults. This service raises crucial issues of love, innocence, aging, and sharing God's Word, that can lead to valuable discussion.
3. Follow service with discussion on theme, "How Am I Witnessing?" Two possibilities would be:
    a. Have each person write on one side of 3 x 5 card their thoughts on — "How I Have Given A Christian Witness This Week." On other side have them write on — "How I Have Failed In My Witness This Week." Invite those who are willing to share with the entire group. Close with service of rededication.
    b. Divide group into diads or triads for sharing of personal experiences on above themes — one at a time. Sharing should lead to support of each other in daily witness.
4. Use this service as first of series on evangelism. As children share their faith in this service (children write notes on cards and launch balloons), it will challenge adults to consider their Christian witness. Challenge them further with next worship service and lead them to deeper commitment. A successful visitation evangelism program can follow.

Halloween — From Goblins to Saints

Theme of the Service

Halloween, today, is a celebration for children. It is a time of costuming and false identities, a time of tricking and treating, a time of UNICEF-ing. But have you ever noticed the fun that adults have on Halloween? Granted there are those persons who can only reflect upon the work of concocting costumes, or those persons whose image of self-importance will not allow them to dress up or dress down. But remember those adults who were witches, ghosts, or clowns on Halloween night. How they enjoyed sharing in the fun and the excitement.

In addition, Halloween is the eve of All Saints Day (All Hallows Eve). It is a time when we might well be reminded of the courageous men and women who have served God within the world. This program is designed to celebrate Halloween as we generally observe it and then celebrate the saints, pointing to All Saints Day within the calendar of the church. The program consists of the celebration of un-masking followed by the celebration of the saints.

Directions for the Celebration

Publicity

This celebration should not only be advertised, but promoted and sold to the congregation. Small masks, and small cut-outs of St. Francis, could be created as hand-outs advertising the celebration. Children could be encouraged to visit other church school classes to talk about it. For additional promotion, one person could be in costume (clown or hobo) and visit the various classrooms. On the three preceding Sundays, have one person come in costume to the worship service to promote it. He could explain the purpose of the celebration, the meaning of All Saints Day, the relationahip of All Hallows Eve to All Saints Day, the schedule for the celebration, and the importance of having adults, youth, and children involved. This person could talk, use signs, pantomime, magic, or have an interpreter speak for him. It is extremely important to create curiosity, interest, and the awareness that this is a legitimate experience for all ages.

The Halloween Party
The directions are given along with the description of the activity on the following pages.

The All Saints Service
In order for this service to be effective, an advance rehearsal is a must. It must flow smoothly from one section to another with each participant knowing just what he is to do and when. Bulletins will be necessary for the unison and responsive sections.

It will be helpful to use a large number of persons in this service. For example, have a different person give each of the readings from the writings of the saints. Alternate light and dark voices if possible; also have the readings given from different sections of the sanctuary rather than all from the chancel. Likewise, each story of a saint should be presented by a different person. These stories should not be read, but told in the words of the one giving the presentation.

The service is designed to be held in the sanctuary and could be held on the Sunday preceding or following All Saints Day. Persons may attend dressed in their costumes, with the exception of the masks. If so, then the various readers should also wear their costumes.

Materials/People Needed

The Halloween Party

1. Straw, or hay (about 12 bales broken open to create pile)
2. Pumpkins
3. String (for marshmallows)
4. Felt scraps
5. Assorted magic markers
6. Cardboard boxes of various sizes (at least 20 — dress boxes, soap boxes, refrigerator boxes, etc.)
7. Tempera paint (powder base — at least 3 colors)
8. Paint brushes and buckets
9. String (at least 10 pieces — each 7 feet long)
10. Old magazines (to cut for pictures)
11. Paper (for mobiles)
12. Wire and string (for mobiles)
13. Amplification equipment
14. Records or tapes
15. Glue (strong fast-drying)
16. Area co-ordinators

The All Saints Service

1. Organist
2. Ushers (to distribute bulletins)
3. Leader
4. Readers (at least four)
5. Story-tellers (at least three)
6. Choir (optional)
7. Bulletins
8. Hymnals
9. Resource books (for children's stories)
    a. Politi, Leo, Saint Francis and the Animals, Charles Scribner's Sons, New York, 1959.
    b. Langstaff, John, St. George and the Dragon, McClelland & Stewart, Ltd., Canada, 1973.
    c. Spicer, Dorothy Gladys, 13 Jolly Saints, Coward-McCann, Inc., New York, 1970.

    d. Cornelius, Sister Mary, *Fifteen Saints for Girls*, Bruce Publishing Co., Milwaukee, 1951.

    e. Williamson, Hugh Ross, *The Young People's Book of Saints*, Hawthorn Books Inc., New York, 1960.

10. Resource books (for readings from the saints)

    a. Kepler, Thomas S., *The Fellowship of the Saints*, Abingdon-Cokesbury, New York, 1958.

    b. Kepler, Thomas S., *A Journey With the Saints*, World Publishing Co., Cleveland, 1951.

    c. Potts, J. Manning, *Listening to the Saints*, The Upper Room, Nashville, 1962.

The Halloween Party

The area for this activity should be arranged before any participants arrive. The area co-ordinators should be prepared to supervise their particular activity. Music should be playing as the first costumed participants arrive.

The Straw Pile

The pile of straw, or hay, should be in an area by itself. Allow persons plenty of room to jump, throw straw, and roll. The supervisor (s) will want to limit the number of persons in the pile at any one time. In addition, persons should not be permitted to remain too long in/on the pile. Finally, the straw should not be carried away from the pile to other interest areas.

The Web

The supervisor of this activity needs to do plenty of work ahead of time. Ten pieces of string (each piece seven feet long) are tangled and woven together. Only the ends of the string extend out of the web. Participants tie one end of string to one wrist. If you use ten lengths of string, you will need twenty persons. It is important that the string be tied firmly around the persons' wrists. The task is to find one's partner by becoming disentangled from the web. Of course, the string cannot be broken. Persons will find it necessary to climb around and through the web to find their partner and release their length of string. The first team which is released from the web is the winner. Be prepared with many webs; this is a popular activity.

Marshmallow Race

One marshmallow is placed in the center of a string four feet long. Two persons place each end of the string in their mouths and try to reach the marshmallow by pulling the string into their mouths with their tongues. Do not use hands. Have a number of sets prepared.

Cardboard Sculpture

Cardboard boxes of assorted sizes should be in a jumbled pile. Participants are to paint the boxes and then create a sculpture. There should be plenty of string and fast-drying glue available to enable persons to place boxes at angles, create overhangs, etc. This activity will need plenty of space.

Mobiles

A Love and Joy mobile can be a creative challenge. Perhaps persons will want to create small mobiles, or a single large one. They can cut pictures from magazines, or draw and paint figures for the mobiles. The finished products should then be hung in the church.

Parade

The parade should be organized after everyone has arrived and persons have participated in many of the activities. The group should parade around the church and, if possible, the neighborhood.

When the parade is completed, individuals should be asked to pair up for the un-masking. If at all possible, children and youth should select adults for partners, rather than other children or youth. They should walk together or find a quiet place to talk.

Some topics the two might discuss are:
1. The thing I enjoyed most at this party.
2. How I feel being in costume and wearing a mask.
3. Could you recognize any persons?

After awhile the two should remove their masks. If they don't know one another, introductions should be made. They might talk about how it feels to take off the mask. Then the two can return to the church for the service of worship.

—Ralph E. Dessem
— D. Gary Klempnauer

THE ALL SAINTS SERVICE

THE HYMN OF PRAISE   "Come, Christians, Join to Sing"

THE LITANY OF CONFESSION

Leader: We have played and laughed together, not knowing our partner or neighbor behind his mask. It was easy to forget the needs of others in the group and how we have treated them.

People: We are one body in Christ, and individually members one of another. (Romans 12:5)

Leader: We have been hiding behind masks, so that others might not know our true identity — our real selves filled with sin and evil.

People: The sins of some men are conspicuous, but the sins of others appear later . . . they cannot remain hidden. (1 Timothy 5:24, 25)

Leader: We have desired to become anonymous, losing our real selves that others might not see us as we really are.

People: For all have sinned and fall short of the glory of God. (Romans 3:23)

Leader: We have tried to hide from God, failing to realize that he sees us in our spiritual nakedness

— sinners who have called themselves Christians.

People: Man looks on the outward appearance, but the Lord looks on the heart. (1 Samuel 16:7)

THE CALL TO CONFESSION (in unison)

O Lord my God, give ear unto my prayer, and let thy mercy harken unto my desire; Thou seest my heart, that so it is. For I am poor and needy, Thou rich to all that call upon Thee. O Lord my God, strength of the strong; hearken unto my soul and hear it crying out of the depths. Let me confess unto Thee . . . and hear the voice of praise, and drink-in Thee, and meditate on the wonderful things out of thy law; even from the beginning, wherein Thou madest the heaven and the earth, unto the everlasting reigning of thy holy city with Thee. Amen.

— from Book XI, *The Confessions*
St. Augustine (354-430)

THE SILENT PRAYERS OF CONFESSION

THE WORDS OF ASSURANCE

THE AFFIRMATION OF FAITH   The Apostles Creed

THE STORIES OF THE SAINTS (for children present)
St. Francis

Francis was a young man who lived in Italy near the end of the twelfth century. The people in his town of Assisi were angry with the people in a near-by town and they were fighting one another. One day, Francis was captured by men from the enemy town. They kept him in jail — away from home — for a year.

Francis was very lonely. He dreamed of home and all the things he could do there — the things he could eat and the places he could go. When the fight between the two towns ended, Francis was freed and sent home. But things had changed during the fighting, and he was not happy at home.

But while he was at home he had a dream that he was to serve God. Francis vowed he would do this as best he could. He saw persons who were sick and began to help them. He discovered others who were hungry and found food for them. People came to love the holy man, Francis, and they came to trust him. The birds and animals would come to him for he did not make them afraid. He would just stretch out his hand and help all the animals and persons who would come to him. Francis became known as a man who loved and served others in God's name.

St. George

George was a young tribune, living in the fourth century. He was loyal to the emperor Diocletian. When the emperor began to persecute the Christians, George criticized him publicly and he angrily resigned from the army.

Some emperors think they are very important; Diocletian thought he was extremely important. He was not going to allow some young man to criticize him and not be punished. So the soldiers followed young George — and one night they found him and cut his head off!

There were many people who admired young George. They thought he was a remarkable person for standing up for his beliefs. As people gathered — telling about the unusual bravery of young George they began talking about Diocletian — the fire-breathing dragon. Soon stories spread over the country of how George did battle with the dragon. George did fight the emperor — and some might think that was even worse than fighting a dragon.

The important thing for us to remember is that George is famous for his bravery and for his determination to be fair to other persons and loyal to God.

St. Patrick

A young Roman boy of 16 was captured by pirates and sold into slavery in Ireland in the fifth century. All the hair was shaved off his head, so everyone would know that he was a slave. His job was to watch the pigs! But one day he escaped and found his way to France where he received his education. He was determined that he would become a priest. Eventually he went to Rome where he received further training. While there, he convinced the Pope to form a mission in Ireland and Patrick was placed in charge of it.

When he returned to Ireland, Patrick learned that all the chiefs of the country had been summoned by the king for a feast at Tara. The day before the feast, all the lights of Tara were to be put out until the priests of the king would light the holy fire.

Patrick reached a point across the valley from Tara; there he lighted a fire which was seen by the king and all his priests. When the priests looked into the distance and saw the fire, they declared: "O king, this fire is in opposition to your decree and is in opposion to you. It must be put out *now* — or it will burn forever." Though the king and his priests drew near to Patrick, they were unable to frighten him — nor were they able to put out the fire.

The next day the king invited Patrick to his court. There Patrick talked with the king about God, Christ, and the Christian faith. In an effort to explain God as Father, Son and Holy Ghost, he plucked a three leaf clover and said, "As this clover is three and yet one, so God is three: Father, Son and Holy Ghost, but yet one."

Patrick continued to work in Ireland and he became famous for his miraculous accomplishments.

THE SCRIPTURE (paraphrase)   Ephesians 4:11-16

And Christ's gifts were that some should be apostles, some prophets, some evangelists, some pastors and teachers so that the saints together make a unity in the work of service, building up the body of Christ. Thus all of us are to come to unity in our faith and knowledge of Christ. We are not full personhood, the maturity of Christ. We are not meant to be children tossed about with every wind of doctrine, by the cunning of deceitful persons. Rather, speaking the truth in love, we are called to grow up in every way into the one who is the head, into Christ, from whom the whole body, every joint adding its own particular strength, grows until it has built itself up in love.

THE AFFIRMATION OF CHRIST'S PRESENCE

Left Side	*Right Side*
Christ be with me	Christ within me
Christ behind me	Christ before me
Christ beside me	Christ to win me
Christ to comfort	and restore me
Christ beneath me	Christ above me
Christ in quiet	Christ in danger

All

Christ in the hearts of all that love me,
Christ in mouth of friend and stranger.

— from *St. Patrick's Breastplate*
St. Patrick (fifth century)

THE HYMN OF FAITH   "Faith of Our Fathers"

LISTENING TO THE SAINTS

Words of Admonition

Consider, O man, how great the excellence in which the Lord has placed you because He has created and formed you to the image of his beloved Son according to the body and to his own likeness according to the spirit. And all the creatures that are under heaven serve and know and obey their Creator in their own way better than you.

If you were so clever and wise that you possessed all science, and if you knew how to interpret every form of language and to investigate heavenly things minutely, you could not glory in all this, because one demon has known more of heavenly things and still knows more of earthly things than all men, although there may be some man who has received a special knowledge of sovereign wisdom. In like manner, if you were handsomer and richer than all others, and even if you could work wonders and put the demons to flight, all these things are hurtful to you and in nowise belong to you, and in them you cannot glory; that, however, in which we may glory is in our infirmities, and in bearing daily the holy cross of our Lord Jesus Christ.

Let us all consider the Good Shepherd who to save his sheep bore the suffering of the cross. The sheep of the Lord followed him in tribulation and persecution and shame, in hunger and thirst, in infirmity and temptations and in all other ways; and for these things they have received everlasting life from the Lord. Wherefore, it is a great shame for us, the servants of God, that, whereas the saints have practiced works, we should expect to receive honor and glory for reading and preaching the same.

— selected from writings of
Francis of Assisi (1182 - 1226)

A *Godly Meditation* (written from prison)
Give me thy grace, good Lord,
To set the world at nought,
To set my mind fast upon thee.
And not to hang upon the blast of men's mouths.
To be content to be solitary,

Not to long for worldly company
Little and little utterly to cast off the world,
And rid my mind of all the business thereof.
Gladly to be thinking of God
Piteously to call for his help,
To lean upon the comfort of God,
Busily to labor to love him.

> — from *A Godly Meditation*
> Sir Thomas More (1478 - 1535)

On Meditation (Consideration)

Do you ask what piety is? It is leaving time for consideration. You may perhaps tell me that herein I differ from him who defines piety as "the worship of God." I do not really differ from him . . . What is so essential to the worship of God as the practice to which he (God) exhorts in the Psalm, "Be still and know that I am God." This certainly is the chief object of consideration. Is anything, in all respects, so influential, as consideration? Does it not by a kindly anticipation create the divisions of the active life itself, in a manner rehearsing and arranging beforehand what has to be done? There must be consideration lest haply affairs which foreseen and premeditated might turn out well, may if percipitated, be fraught with peril . . .

First of all, consideration purifies the very fountain, that is the mind, from which it springs. Then it governs the affections, directs our actions, corrects excesses, softens the manners, adorns and regulates the life, and lastly bestows the knowledge of things divine and human alike. It is consideration that brings order out of disorder, puts in the links, pulls things together, investigates mysteries, traces the truth, weighs probabilities, exposes shams and counterfeits. It is consideration which arranges beforehand what is to be done, and ponders what is accomplished, so that nothing faulty, or needing correction may settle in the mind. It is consideration which in prosperity feels the sting of adversity, in adversity is as though it felt not.

— from *On Consideration*
Bernard of Clairvaux (1090 - 1153)

The Habit of the Presence of God

From my entering upon a religious life, I have looked upon God as the end of all thoughts and affections of my soul. In the beginning of my novitiate, during the time appointed for public prayer, I labored to be convinced of the truth and reality of this Divine Being, rather by the light of faith than by the labor of meditations and long reasoning: And by this short and certain method, I advanced in the knowledge of this amiable Object, in whose presence I resolve to abide forever. Thus penetrated with the greatness of this infinite Being, I shut myself up in the place where my duty called me, which was the kitchen. I was there alone; and when I had provided everything necessary for my office, I employed the rest of my time in prayer, both before and after my ordinary labor.

When I began anything, I said to God with a filial confidence: My God since thou art with me, and it is by thy appointment I must apply my mind to these external things; I beg thou mayest give me grace to continue with Thee. And that I may act the better, labor with me, O Lord, receive my words and possess all my affections. In fine, during my daily tasks, I continued to speak familiarly to God, to offer Him all my little services, and to demand his grace. When the action was over, I considered what way I had done it. If I found it was well done, I thanked God for it. If it was amiss, I begged his forgiveness. Thus, without being discouraged, I rectified my mind; and returned again into God's presence, as if I had never wandered from it.

Thus rising up still after my falls, and multiplying acts of faith and love, I am come to such a state, that it would be as little possible for me not to think on God, as it was difficult to get myself used to it in the beginning.

—from *The Practice of the Presence of God*
Nicholas Herman (Brother Lawrence 1611-1691)

THE CLOSING HYMN   "For All the Saints"

THE PRAYER OF DEDICATION (in unison)
    Lord, make me an instrument of your peace.
    Where there is hatred . . . let me sow love.
    Where there is injury . . . pardon.
    Where there is doubt . . . faith.
    Where there is despair . . . hope.
    Where there is darkness . . . light.
    Where there is sadness . . . joy.

    O Divine Master, grant that I may not so much seek
    To be consoled . . . as to console,
    To be understood . . . as to understand,
    To be loved . . . as to love,
        for
    It is in giving . . . that we receive,
    It is in pardoning . . . that we are pardoned,
    It is in dying . . . that we are born to eternal life.

—St. Francis of Assisi

THE BENEDICTION

—Ralph E. Dessem
—D. Gary Klempnauer

ADDITIONAL IDEAS
1. A light dinner could be served and become a bridge between the two activities.

2. The leader could develop the idea that we have saints in our church today. Participants could be asked to think about persons in the congregation who are special. They could be asked to give the names of such persons at a special point in the service.
3. The readers, who present the messages for the saints, could be asked to dress in costumes which would represent their particular saints.
4. This celebration could be done at a location other than a church, such as a camp site. However, it would be important to stress that persons come in costumes.
5. One or two women could be included in the presentation of the saints — both in the story and message sections. (See resource books for material on this.)
6. Form a study group to read and discuss the writings of some of the saints. This would be good to either precede or follow the celebration.
7. Have group make set of large posters to place on display in the church. Each poster should have a picture and a quotation of a specific saint.

The King is Coming

Theme of the Service

The theme of any Advent service ought to be to prepare the participants for the celebration of the birth of the Christ-child. This liturgical celebration goes even farther, as it draws a parallel to the coming of the King into the city of Jerusalem on Palm Sunday. Thus, it follows the current theological emphasis of the church year for the beginning of Advent.

A most important aspect of this service is involvement. Children are involved as well as youth and adults. It is the type of worship experience that will be remembered for a long time -- by each member of the family.

Directions for the Service

The congregation did not have the entire script before them when this service was first conducted at Asbury United Methodist Church in Delaware, Ohio. The bulletin contained only that which was necessary for them to follow and participate. To have this entire service in hand would involve the congregation with too much reading and seriously cripple the effect of the service.

Detailed directions are given throughout the service and need to be followed closely to result in an effective worship experience. The importance of several rehearsals beforehand cannot be overemphasized.

One of the keys to the effectiveness of this service lies in the choice of the four readers and their presentation. They must put feeling into their words or the service will drag. They should be chosen with thought given to alternation of light and dark voices.

The music is also very important and several choirs can be used to present the anthems. The ideal would be to use three groups — one each of children, youth, and adults.

The dancers need to be experienced and have their presentation well rehearsed. Everyone will be watching them, since this is not done in most churches every Sunday.

Careful preparations need to be made for the Advent activity. Have enough pine branches so that each child can carry one to the chancel and lay it on the steps. Likewise, have sufficient straw so that each member of this group has some to carry. The cross should be quite large, so that it takes several persons to carry it. Place it against the chancel wall at one side of the altar. The star can be placed on the other side of the altar. This should be quickly attached to a wire already in place.

Materials/People needed
1. Four readers
2. Two or three choirs
3. Minister
4. Ushers (prayer given to one)
5. Acolyte (Advent candle)
6. Dancers (three, preferably)
7. Complete scripts (for all participants)
8. Hymns:
    "Joy to the World"
    "Wake, Awake for Night is Flying"
    "O Come, O Come, Emmanuel"
9. Anthems:
    "Rejoice Greatly" — Johannes Petzold
    "Joy to the World" — Ronald Nelson
    "Wake, O Shepherds" — J. Philippe Rameau
    "Carol for Epiphany"
    "And Lo, the Star" — Johannes Petzold
    "Now Tell Us, Gentle Mary — French Carol
10. Pine branches
11. Small crib
12. Straw
13. Large wood cross
14. Large glittery star

THE SERVICE

PRELUDE

SCRIPTURE SENTENCES [by minister from rear of sanctuary]
[Advent candle lighted during reading]
Rejoice greatly, O daughter of Zion
Shout aloud, O daughter of Jerusalem!
Lo, your king comes to you;
triumphant and victorious is he,
humble and riding on an ass,
on a colt the foal of an ass. (Zechariah 9:9)

PROCESSIONAL ANTHEM "Rejoice Greatly" Johannes Petzold

INVITATION INTO THE COMPANY [Read from among congregation]
1st R.: Children of Israel, Community of Christ:
We, God's wayward children, are called now and yesterday and all tomorrow, in every single instant of our eating, sleeping, playing, working, fighting, loving, hoping, and despairing lives. We are called to be actors in the Company of the King. It is an honor to be called, although the play is difficult. Today our company starts a new year together as we begin to prepare the stage for the birth of the baby Jesus.
2nd R.: But how do we begin?
3rd R: We've been here before, yet it's never the same.
1st R.: It isn't easy. For we're not asked to tell history, to give some accurate portrayal of past events defined by time and space. But from the gospel story we must find pattern and direction, and then we ourselves create activity and script.

We have an ancient shape or movement which calls for actions always new.

4th R.: What does it mean to prepare for this birth?

3rd R.: We need to know the man before we make way for the child.

1st R.: That's right. The babe's triumphal humble entry into this crazy human world starts to take on meaning only as we move triumphantly with Jesus into the Holy City of Jerusalem and shout aloud with all the crowd, "Hosanna to the Son of David! Blessed be he who comes in the name of the Lord!" We must be present for the days of confrontation, be learning from the teacher prophet Jesus the image, shape and stance of life, eat with him, be with him, and follow — to that agonizing death upon the cross.

2nd R.: Where's the light? We can't act without the light.

1st R.: Light?

The cross — the impact of this man's death experienced as new life — is the light in which we actors move. It is the morning sun of Easter, Epiphany's bright star. We cannot do the play without the light. So, actors, to do the play we must stay in the light for *all* the action! The play is a story of new creation,

3rd R.: new story bursting forth out of the old,

4th R.: new life springing from death,

2nd R.: new light shattering darkness,

3rd R.: awakeness dispelling sleep,

4th R.: It is the story of the coming of the kingdom of God . . . through death . . . and the birth of a baby.

1st R.: We have the light, and image, style, direction. The script we must create. The movement is a dance of joy through sorrow unto death and life. Remember, actors, when we are in the light and on the stage, even sitting still is action; we must always be involved. Concentrate. Be fully there for one another in the name of Christ, Director-King. We are a company of actors, each one essential to the others. Do not be misled into thinking that the actor who at one moment is called upon to run or dance or speak is more important than the one who waits and listens and is still. Nor can an actor on the stage pretend to be attentive in the action while in reality he dreams or sleeps. Every actor sometimes stumbles, drops a line, or unsurely hesitates. There is forgiveness, but there is no time for fakery. The play demands involvement of the total human being. Each stance or move must help complete a total action of the company.

2nd R.: [Going forward] The agony of death is over but will come again. The light encircles us. Let us prepare for the birth of the infant King.

RESPONSIVE READING   Psalms 98
[Alternately led by 2nd and 4th readers; 2nd standing before the congregation, 4th continuing to stand within congregation]

ANTHEM   "Joy to the World"   Ronald Nelson
[The first part of this anthem is to be sung by the choir alone. In the last section, the congregation is invited to join in singing "Joy to the World" from the hymnal. Readers go to rear of sanctuary during singing of hymn.]

A DANCE FOR THE KING [with three dancers]
[Reading is Psalm 98 with inserted Scripture]
Reading Chorus: O Sing to the Lord a new song, for for he has done marvelous things.
1st R.: Rejoice greatly, O daughter of Zion
        Shout aloud, O daughter of Jerusalem!
    Lo, your king comes to you;
        triumphant and victorious is he,

humble and riding on an ass,
       on a colt the foal of an ass.

Chorus: His right hand and his holy arm have gotten him victory.

2nd R.: But you, O Bethlehem, who are little to be among the clan of Judah, from you shall come forth for me one who is to be ruler in Israel . . .

Chorus: He has revealed his vindication in the sight of the nations.

4th R.: Therefore the Lord himself will give you a sign. Behold a woman shall conceive and bear a son, and shall call his name Immanuel, which means God with us.

Chorus: He has remembered his steadfast love and faithfulness to the house of Israel.

2nd R.: Then Herod summoned the wise men, and he sent them to Bethlehem, saying, "Go and search diligently for the child, and when you have found him, bring me word, that I, too, may come and worship him." And going into the house they saw the child with Mary, his mother, and they fell down and worshiped him. Then opening their treasures, they offered him gifts, gold and frankincense and myrrh.

3rd r.: When the centurion and those who were with him keeping watch over Jesus saw the earth-quake and what took place they were filled with awe and said, "Truly this was a Son of God."

Chorus: All the ends of the earth have seen the victory of our God.

1st R.: Lo, your King comes to you, triumphant and victorious is he, humble and riding on an ass.

Chorus: Let the floods clap their hands;
       Let the hills sing for joy together before the Lord,
       for he comes to judge the earth.

4th R.: The people who walked in darkness have seen a great light.

Chorus: He will judge the world with righteousness, and the peoples with equity.

2nd R.: For unto us a child is born, and his name will be called Wonderful Counselor, Mighty God, Everlasting Father, Prince of Peace.

4th R.: And this will be a sign for you: you will find a babe wrapped in swaddling clothes and lying in a manger.

3rd R.: And plaiting a crown of thorns they put it on his head, and put a reed in his right hand. And kneeling before him they mocked him, saying, "Hail, King of the Jews!" And they spat upon him and took the reed and struck him on the head. and when they had mocked him they stripped him of the robe, and put his own clothes on him, and led him away to crucify him.

Chorus: He will judge the world with righteousness, and the peoples with equity.

1st R.: Rejoice greatly . . . shout aloud . . . your king comes to you . . . triumphant . . . victorious . . . humble . . . and riding on an ass.

2nd R.: For unto us a child is born.

3rd R.: Now as they were eating, Jesus took bread, and blessed, and broke it and gave it to the disciples and said, "Take, eat; this is my body." And he took the cup, and when he had given thanks, he gave it to them, saying, "Drink of it, all of you; for this is my blood of the covenant, which is poured out for many for the forgiveness of sins."

Chorus: Make a joyful noise to the Lord, all the earth;
break forth into joyous song and sing praises!
Sing praises to the Lord with the lyre,
with the lyre and the sound of melody!
With trumpets and the sound of the horn
make a joyful noise before the King, the Lord!

Let the sea roar, and all that fills it;
the world and those who dwell in it.

1st R.: Lo, your king comes to you triumphant and victorious.

Chorus: Make a joyful noise before the King, the Lord!

[Readers immediately start forward, down the aisles, joyfully shouting "Advent" to the people, overlapping one another in sound and building to crescendo! Beginning of hymn interrupts readers who seat themselves among congregation.]

HYMN   "Wake, Awake for Night is Flying"

SCRIPTURE   1 Thessalonians 5:1-10

2nd R.: There is no need to write you about the times and occasions when these things will happen. For you, yourselves, know very well that the Day of the Lord will come like a thief comes at night.

4th R.: When people say, "Everything is quiet and safe," then suddenly destruction will hit them! They will not escape — it will be like the pains that come upon a woman who is about to give birth.

3rd R.: But you are not in the darkness, and the Day should not take you by surprise like a thief. All of you are people who belong to the light, who belong to the day. We are not of the night or of darkness. So then, we should not be sleeping like the others; we should be awake and sober.

2nd R.: It is at night when people sleep; it is at night when people get drunk. But we belong to the day, and we should be sober.

4th R.: We must wear faith and love as a breastplate, and our hope of salvation as a helmet.

Minister: God did not choose us to suffer his wrath, but to possess salvation through our Lord Jesus Christ, who died for us in order that we might live together with him, whether we are alive or dead when he comes.

LITANY OF DESPAIR AND HOPE

[*Leader, 3rd reader, stands in front of congregation. Other readers remain seated.*]

3rd R.: We must prepare for the King. When will he come?

People: The Day of the Lord will come as a thief comes at night.

3rd R.: Listen . . .

1st R.: Advent
   Of what?
   Great burst of hope, utopian dreams come true?
   No more bombs, no more riots, no more crime,
   No more foul despoiling of the earth and air,
   No more rats or bloated bellies
   No more violence
   No more hate
   No more bondage to our misconceptions of ourselves and one another?

3rd R.: What safe place is there for the birth of a baby? Where can a star shine?

People: Lo, your king comes to you, triumphant and victorious is he, humble and riding on an ass.

3rd R.: You know the world we live in. Can you believe in a King?

People: The Day of the Lord will come as a thief comes at night.

3rd R.: Listen . . .

2nd R.: Another year. Another Advent.
   And we wait in the chaos of this alien world for what? A fairy tale of shepherds and a baby King? For Godot who never comes? See your

people, God, waiting through cold rain, bitter tears, falling bombs, with horror in our hearts, so inadequate to soothe and heal this wounded, dying world.

3rd R.: Is there a place to find shepherds at the birth of a King?

People: Lo, your king comes to you, triumphant and victorious is he, humble and riding on an ass.

3rd R.: Who can believe today in a King?

People: The Day of the Lord will come as a thief comes at night.

3rd R.: Listen . . .

4th R.: Advent.

We don't know how to wait for the baby, to prepare for the king, and there really isn't time. There is so much to do before Christmas. Still, shopping is hectic, but sometimes fun. And evergreens make houses smell fresh and exciting. And candle-lit evenings with family, friends and good food bring moments of peace.

3rd R.: Is there time or a place for the child to be born?

People: Lo, your king comes to you, triumphant and victorious is he, humble and riding on an ass.

3rd R.: Listen . . .

2nd R.: Advent.

Tell us a candlelight story in the glow of the Christmas tree. Gunfire. Screams of pain. And death. A child starving in his father's arms. God's people, lonely, poor, heart-broken and oppressed, searching murky sky for sign of a star.

3rd R.: Is there space for a star to shine?

People: Lo, your king comes to you, triumphant and victorious is he, humble and riding on an ass.

3rd R.:

The infant Jesus grew to be a man. He was nailed to the cross and died, that we might have life.

People: The Day of the Lord will come as a thief comes at night.

PRAYER OF PREPARATION

[*With time for prayers of the congregation. Readers remain seated.*]

4th R.: Dear God,

How can we act in view of all the odds? Our speech cannot be heard above the angry shouts and dropping bombs. We've forgotten or we never knew how we should dance

across a battleground of dead,

through city streets of broken glass,

through neighborhoods of hate and fear —

or in the lives of those we love.

Gestures cannot easily take shape or words communicate in this world of broken meanings. We read the story, but we cannot understand the stage directions any more. How can we move? We're in no condition now to act — slack muscles, sleepy heads. We are distracted in a thousand busy ways. Surrounded by thick smog of apathy, frustration, fear, we cannot see the light around us, or each other. In the name of God, how on earth can we prepare for the birth of this child?

Minister: Paul said, "God did not choose us to suffer his wrath, but to possess salvation through our Lord Jesus Christ, who died for us in order that we might live together with him, whether we are alive or dead when he comes. For this reason, encourage one another and help one another just as you are now doing."

1st R.: Can we speak to one another of preparation for the baby's birth? The play is old, the world is sick. Is it possible today to dance for the King? Let us share our prayers of sorrow and hope. What prayers will you now offer?

[*Prayers of congregation, silent and audible*]
2nd R.: Advent.
    Birth of Wonder?
    Birth of Love?
    In this sick world of hate and fear?
1st R.: Yes. Christ Jesus made it happen once and
    and every moment still.
3rd R.: Act the play.
4th R.: Dance for him.
3rd R.: Old worlds die.
4th R.: New worlds are born.
2nd R.: Even here, even now,
1st R.: New life from death. Amen.

HYMN   "O Come, O Come Emmanuel"

ANNOUNCEMENTS
    1st R.: [*Walking among congregation*]
    When it is time to offer to the King our money,
    it is a worthy thing to do. But to act with one part
    of ourselves is not enough. It is like sitting on
    stage with simulated rapt attention to the total
    action, while day-dreaming all the time of sleep.
    It breaks the interaction, spoils the scene.
    Remember — all our action must be total and
    within the light, and our work, our play, our
    thought, our love, our art, our festivals and
    celebrations must be ever new but all moving
    with the play's design.

        Our moments here together should be times
    of sharing and of celebration — rehearsals, in a
    way, but really not. In importance these times
    are no more nor less a part of our playing for the
    King. In these gathered moments we should
    build each other up and find special ways to
    bring the play alive.
    2nd R.: [*Going to front of church*]
    Let's begin to set the stage for the baby's birth!

SCRIPTURE   Matthew 21:1-9
  [*Read by 2nd Reader, standing before congregation*]

ADVENT ACTIVITY
1st R.: [*Standing*]
   Jesus is coming into Jerusalem. Who will help to lay
   down branches for him?
   [*1st Reader gathers children from the choir,
   takes them to a side of the church where there is
   greenery, gives each child a branch and
   instructs the children to lay branches on wide
   steps between altar rails. Children sit on either
   side in aisle in front of altar rail.*]
2nd R.: [*Standing*]
   The road to Jerusalem leads to the cross. Who
   will help me to carry the cross?
   [*2nd Reader gathers several memebers of
   congregation, who carry the cross from the back
   of the church, and place it behind the greenery.
   These persons sit, or kneel, like the children.*]
3rd R.: [*Standing*]
   Now it is time for the birth. Who will help me to
   carry the crib and the straw?
   [*3rd Reader gathers helpers, who bring the crib
   and straw from another point in the rear of the
   sanctuary, and set the crib upon the greenery,
   and fill it with straw. They also sit or kneel.*]
4th R.: [*Standing*]
   The star shines over Bethlehem. Who will help
   me to let it be seen?
   [*4th Reader gathers helpers who bring a large
   glittery star. It is hung on a wire high above the
   altar.*]
1st R.: [*Motioning for the entire congregation to
   stand*]
   These acts of preparation affirm the coming of
   our King. Let us now shout together, Glory to
   God in the Highest!

[*Response*]
Shout Hallelujah!
[*Response*]
Say Amen!
[*Response, after which people are seated*]

SCRIPTURE   Luke 2:8-15
[*Read by 4th Reader, standing before congregation*]

ANTHEM   "Wake, O Shepherds"   J. Phillippe Rameau

SCRIPTURE   Matthew 2:1-11
[*Read by 3rd Reader, standing before congregation*]

OFFERTORY ANTHEM   "Carol for Epiphany"
[*Offering collected in gift-wrapped boxes during
anthem, ushers moving from rear to front of church.*]

OFFERTORY PRAYER
[*Ushers kneel before crib, place gifts there and one
offers prayer*]
Dear God,
We are like wise men kneeling at the manger bed.
Bringing gifts, we receive in turn new hope and joy.
We've traveled far to come into the light — Easter
sun, Epiphany's bright star. Eternal life is new life
screaming to be free. The baby's birth, rebirth of life
and love eternally.
      In the name of the crucified man
      In the name of the infant King. Amen!

ANTHEM   "And Lo, the Star"   Johannes Petzold

SCRIPTURE   Luke 1:26-33
[*Read by 1st Reader, standing before congregation*]

ANTHEM   "Now Tell Us, Gentle Mary"   French Carol
                [*With dance*]

COMMISSION OF THE COMPANY

Minister: For lo, your King comes to you, triumphant and victorious is he, humble, and riding on an ass.

People: The Day of the Lord will come like a thief comes at night.

Minister: Make a joyful noise to the Lord all the earth. Break forth into joyous song and sing praises.

People: Hosanna! Hosanna in the highest! Amen!

2nd R.: Children of Israel,
Community of Christ,
Actors in the Company of the King,
You are in the Light, and you are *the* light.
You are the Light of the World!
Your every thought is act and every act a dance for the King. Go forth with love and thanksgiving, awake, attentive to each other.
Prepare in every way, in all these busy days of work and play, prepare for the birth of your infant King!

Minister: Hosanna in the highest! Amen!

POSTLUDE

— Beth Reed

ADDITIONAL IDEAS

1. Provide the complete text of this Liturgical Celebration to be used in discussion groups after the service. These groups could meet immediately following the service or later in the week.

2. Develop an Advent study using this service as a kick-off. The theological content can provide the basis for the discussion in the study groups.

3. Use this service as your design for Advent. Present the complete service on the first Sunday in Advent.

Follow with segments being repeated on the three remaining Sundays.

4. Adapt the service to your own congregation, but realize that its effectiveness will be limited if the liturgy is changed. For example, if dancers are not available, Psalm 98 (with inserted Scripture) should still be presented by a reading chorus.

Getting Ready for Christmas

Theme of the Service

This service is designed to teach preparation for Christmas worship and the celebration of Jesus' birthday. If it is held on Christmas Eve, as it was in Faith Lutheran Church of Walworth, Wisconsin, it depicts the theme of Advent ending and Christmas beginning. In this particular church, there are no Christmas hymns sung during the Advent season; only those dealing with the Advent message are used. Thus, this congregation is accustomed to Christmas Eve marking a dramatic change in the program of the church.

Informality is emphasized in this service. As children are used to place the various Christmas items in their proper locations, the service becomes quite meaningful to them.

Involvement is also an important aspect of "Getting Ready for Christmas." In addition to the use of some children in placing the items, other children and youth are used in various choirs. Three different choral groups were used in this service when it was presented. Other youth were used as readers. Thus, with the adults joining in singing some of the hymns, all members of the family were involved in this service.

Directions for the Service

Advance preparation is most important for this service to be successful. The choirs, or singing groups, should be well rehearsed. This singing could be done by three different groups of children or youth from the Church School classes, with some of the rehearsal being done in their classes. In the major portion of the service, the various choirs refer to age groups: 1st choir — youngest children, 2nd choir — middle children, 3rd choir — older children. The young persons who serve as readers should be given their Scripture passages several weeks in advance so they can practice.

Make certain everything is "prepared" in terms of the cross not being on the altar, the candles not lighted, and so on. The pastor should make comments about the meaning and purpose of each item, before it is placed in its proper location. He should talk freely with the children as they are gathered in the chancel, asking questions which would lead to the correct answer. (Ex.: "What is missing from the altar?" Answer: "The cross.") Please remember that considerable time will be consumed in talking about and placing the various items. It is not necessary to appoint children in advance to place specific items in their designated locations.

Selected verses of the hymns may be used in the interest of time. It may also be desirable to change some of them since they may not be familiar to the congregation, or music not be available for the choral groups.

The offering can be a very dramatic experience, with everyone taking his gift to the altar. This gift might be in the form of money, food, clothing, toys, etc. Of course, advance announcement will be necessary for persons to come to the service prepared for this aspect of it.

Materials/People needed
1. Pastor
2. Three choral groups.
3. Ten readers (youth)
4. Cross
5. Altar candles
6. Advent candles
7. Altar flowers
8. Paraments
9. Christmas candle
10. Christmas banner
11. Christmas tree lights
12. Festival candles
13. Christmas flowers

14. Hymns: (sung by congregation)
    "Angels We Have Heard on High"
    "O Come, All Ye Faithful"
    "Joy to the World"
    "What Child is This?"
    "Silent Night"
15. Hymns and Songs: (sung by choral groups)
    "Thou Didst Leave Thy Throne"
    "O Light From Age to Age the Same"
    "Light of the Anxious Heart"
    "Children of the Heavenly Father"
    "Good Christian Men, Rejoice"
    "Fling Out the Banner"
    "For the Beauty of the Earth"
    "O Christmas Tree"
    "When Lights Are Lit" —(in *Folk Hymnal*, compiled by Norman Johnson & John W. Peterson, Singspiration, Inc., 1970.)

THE SERVICE

THE PRELUDE [*Christmas tunes by young musicians*]

THE PROCESSIONAL HYMN
                "Angels We Have Heard On High"
            [*sung by congregation*]

GETTING READY FOR CHRISTMAS

INTRODUCTION
    (Pastor invites group of young children to sit around him in the chancel. He stresses the change between Advent and Christmas and the transition taking place tonight. He points out the many items (those in following list) which are not in their proper place. Thus, we are not yet ready for Christmas worship.)

THE CROSS
Scripture   Hebrews 12:1-2
[1st reader]
Hymn   "Thou Didst Leave Thy Throne"
[3rd choir]

CROSS: [Give the cross to a child to place on the altar.]

THE ALTAR CANDLES
Scripture   John 1:1-9
[2nd reader]
Hymn   "O Light From Age To Age The Same"
[3rd Choir]

ALTAR CANDLES: [Have a child light altar candles.]

THE ADVENT CANDLES
Scripture   Isaiah 9:1-2
[3rd reader]
Hymn   "Light Of The Anxious Heart"

ADVENT CANDLES: [Have another child light four advent candles.]

THE ALTAR FLOWERS
Scripture   Isaiah 40:1-8
[4th reader]
Hymn   "Children Of The Heavenly Father"

ALTAR FLOWERS: [Have two children put flowers on altar.]

THE PARAMENTS
Scripture   Revelation 7:9-17
[5th reader]
Hymn   "Good Christian Men, Rejoice"
[2nd and 3rd Choirs]

PARAMENTS: [*Have other children put paraments on altar and pulpit.*]

THE CHRISTMAS CANDLE

Scripture   Isaiah 9:6-7
[*6th reader*]
Hymn   "Joy To The World"
[*Whole Congregation*]
CHRISTMAS CANDLE: [*Have someone light Christmas Candle.*]

THE CHRISTMAS BANNER

Scripture   Psalms 20:1-9
[*7th reader*]
Hymn   "Fling Out The Banner"
[*2nd and 3rd Choirs*]

CHRISTMAS BANNER: [*Have someone hang Christmas Banner.*]

THE CHRISTMAS TREE LIGHTS

Scripture   Luke 2:24-32
[*8th reader*]
Hymn   "O Christmas Tree"

CHRISTMAS TREE: [*Have children light Christmas Tree.*]

THE FESTIVAL CANDLES

Scripture   Luke 11:33-36
[*9th reader*]
Hymn   "When Lights Are Lit"

FESTIVAL CANDLES: [*Have someone light these candles.*]

THE CHRISTMAS FLOWERS

Scripture   Psalms 96:1-12

[*10th reader*]
Hymn   "For The Beauty Of The Earth"
[*sung by all children*]

CHRISTMAS FLOWERS: [*Children place poinsettias.*]

THE CHRISTMAS SCRIPTURE   Luke 2:1-20

THE CHRISTMAS HYMN   "O Come, All Ye Faithful"
[*Sung by congregation*]

THE CHRISTMAS OFFERING
    The Scripture   Romans 15:25-28
    The Hymn   "What Child Is This?"
    [*Sung by entire congregation as everyone walks to
    chancel to give their gifts of money, food, clothing,
    toys, etc.*]

THE CHRISTMAS PRAYER
    The Prayer [*Pastor*]
    The Hymn   "Away In a Manger"
        [*Sung by 1st choir at end of prayer*]

THE BENEDICTION

THE RECESSIONAL HYMN   "Silent Night"
        [*Sung by everyone*]

—Lawrence Ruegg

Additional Ideas
1. This service could be used on the 4th Sunday in
   Advent, especially if it comes within a day or two of
   Christmas.
2. If two Christmas Eve services are usually held in your
   church, this one could be held at an early hour as a
   family service with a more formal one presented
   later.

3. The major portion of the service could be condensed to include less than ten Christmas items; this would permit time for a Christmas sermon.

4. This service could also be shortened by taking the offering in the usual manner. If you have a large congregation, it will take a considerable amount of time for everyone to walk to the altar.

5. If you have a stained glass window of the Nativity, this could be used as one of the ten items. A spotlight could be placed outside and one of the children could press the switch to turn it on.

6. The service could be rearranged so that the "Festival Candles" are lighted at the end of the service. At this point small candles could be lighted by each person.

THE CONTRIBUTORS

Nancy C. Burke is the director of music at Maplewood United Presbyterian Church in Greensburg, Pennsylvania. She is also an airlines reservationist and private voice teacher as well as the director of four youth musical groups. Nancy has attended Muskingum College, Carnegie Mellon University, and Seton Hill College. In working with I. Lee Page, pastor of the Maplewood Church, creative family worship experiences were developed for the congregation; some were recently published in Contagious Celebrations (C.S.S.).

R. Robert Cueni graduated from Kent State University (Ohio) and from Christian Theological Seminary, Indianapolis, Indiana. He is currently working toward his Doctor of Ministry degree through San Francisco Theological Seminary. Along with his wife, Bob has led family camping programs and Marriage Enrichment Seminars. He has served Disciples of Christ churches in Michigan and has just become the pastor of the First Christian Church of Bedford, Indiana. He recently had It Was A Day Like This published by C.S.S.

Ralph E. Dessem graduated from Findlay College and the Oberlin Graduate School of Theology. He received the Doctor of Ministry degree from The Divinity School of Vanderbilt University. Ralph has served several pastorates in northeastern Ohio and is in his fourth year as pastor of the Independence United Methodist Church. He has edited numerous worship materials including A Guide to Contemporary Worship, Contemporary Worship Resources for Special Days and A Season to Return (C.S.S.)

D. Gary Klempnauer is a graduate of DePauw University and Drew Theological Seminary. Having served pastorates in northeastern Ohio, he is in his third year as pastor of the Seven Hills United Methodist Church. Gary has been a camp director and has served as leader of personal growth and conflict management groups; currently he is also Cleveland District chairman of communications. He enjoys writing contemporary worship materials for use in his church.

Robert M. Lautenschlager has served as pastor of the Hope Ridge United Methodist Church, Mentor, Ohio, for the past 20 years. Here he conducts a program which includes experimental efforts in education and worship, as well as various lab and study experiences for youth and adults. Bob is a graduate of Taylor University and Evangelical Theological Seminary, and has taken special training with N.T.L. in Bethel, Maine, and with Reuel Howe's Advanced Pastoral Institute.

I. Lee Page is pastor of the Maplewood United Presbyterian Church in Greensburg, Pennsylvania. He is a graduate of Waynesburg College and Pittsburgh Theological Seminary. For the past seven years he and his music director, Nancy Burke, have developed a variety of worship experiences that have been enthusiastically received by families in the congregation. Twelve of these, using a variety of forms and music, have recently been published by C.S.S. — *Contagious Celebrations.*

Robert L. Randall has been engaged in full time psychotherapy for the past seven years at the Ministry of Counseling Services, located at St. Peter's United Church of Christ, Elmhurst, Illinois. In addition to being an ordained minister, Bob is also a psychologist licensed by the state of Illinois. He graduated from Elmhurst College, Elmhurst, Illinois, and the United Theological Seminary, New Brighton, Minnesota. He has received his M.A. and Ph.D. degrees from the University of Chicago.

Beth Reed is the Coordinator of Women's Studies for the Great Lakes College Association at Ann Arbor, Michigan. She graduated from Otterbein College and has done graduate study at Boston University and the Methodist Theological School in Ohio. Beth enjoys writing liturgy and has produced a district-wide Confirmation Celebration, an All Saints Celebration (involving youth as dancers, singers, actors), and a Service of Holy Communion with jazz (in collaboration with musician, Robert Lepley).

Friedrich Rest is a pastor, presently serving on the staff of the First Protestant United Church of Christ, New Braunfels, Texas. He is a graduate of Elmhurst College and Eden Theological Seminary, and has received his Doctor of Divinity degree. Fred has served on the Commission on Worship of the United Church of Christ. He has written for periodicals as well as books of his own. His publications include: *Our Christian Symbols*, *The Cross in Hymns* and *Our Christian Worship from Palm Sunday through Easter* (C.S.S.).

Lawrence Ruegg has been pastor of Faith Lutheran Church, Walworth Wisconsin, for over twenty years. He graduated from Carthage College and Northwestern Lutheran Theological Seminary. Larry has served on several synod committees and is presently a member of the Synod Executive Board (LCA). His numerous published writings include: *Color Me Healthy, Jesus* (C.S.S.), *God Came Thrice, When You are in the Hospital, You Are Not Alone* and *A Moment With God* (family devotional).

Keith L. Scott graduated from Cornell College (Iowa) and Drew Theological Seminary. He has served churches in Iowa and is currently pastor of Wesley United Methodist Church in Mason City. Keith has been involved in various district and conference activities, and served as Conference Director of Youth Ministries for the North Iowa Conference (U.M.) for four years. He is chairman of the Board of Evangelism and Worship of the Iowa Conference, and program director of the North Iowa Bible Conference.

Judy Gattis Smith is the wife of a United Methodist pastor; she and her husband serve a church in Roanoke, Virginia. Judy received her degree in education from Peabody College (Nashville) and has done graduate work at Julliard School of Music in New York. She has written numerous church dramas and curriculum material for the United Methodist Church, as well as two resource books for church school teachers. Her latest book, *Come Children, Praise and Pray* (C.S.S.), includes twelve liturgies for use with children.